VGM Opportunities Series

OPPORTUNITIES IN
PUBLISHING CAREERS

Robert A. Carter
S. William Pattis

Revised by
Blythe Camenson

Foreword by
Linda Roghaar
Linda Roghaar Literary Agency, Inc.
Amherst, MA

 **VGM Career Books**
NTC/Contemporary Publishing Group

Cover photograph by © Telegraph Colour Library/FPG International

Published by VGM Career Books
A division of NTC/Contemporary Publishing Group, Inc.
4255 West Touhy Avenue, Lincolnwood (Chicago), Illinois 60712-1975 U.S.A.
Copyright © 2001 by NTC/Contemporary Publishing Group, Inc.
International Standard Book Number: 0-658-00483-2 (cloth)
                                     0-658-00484-0 (paper)

01   02   03   04   05   06   LB   15   14   13   12   11   10   9   8   7   6   5   4   3

CONTENTS

Publishing's allied groups. An overview of types of publishers. Trade
book publishing. Regional/small presses. Religion publishing. Textbook
publishing. Technical, scientific, special interest, and medical publishing.
University presses. Organizational/sponsored presses. Paperback
publishing. Mail-order publishing and book clubs. Book packagers/
producers. Subsidy and cooperative publishing. Electronic publishing.

The climate of book publishing. Personal qualifications. Personal
requirements. Women in publishing.

College majors. Professional training programs. Getting started. Salaries
and unions.

The publisher. The editor. The copy editor. The designer. Production and
manufacturing jobs. Sales representatives. School and library sales.

ABOUT THE AUTHORS

Robert A. Carter is a writer, educator, and marketing consultant with wide and intensive publishing experience. He has served on the faculty of Pace University, where he helped create Pace's Master of Science Program in Publishing; at Hofstra University; and at New York University, where for six years he directed the Summer Publishing Institute. He is a frequent lecturer on publishing topics at other colleges and universities. He also has been a contributing editor to *Publishers Weekly,* the international magazine of book publishing, for ten years.

During his distinguished publishing career, Mr. Carter worked for such firms as Doubleday, McGraw-Hill, and as director of publications for the Museum of Modern Art in New York City. In addition he served as an account supervisor for ten years at Franklin Spier, the leading book publishing advertising agency.

His published books include *Manhattan Primitive,* a novel; *Opportunities in Book Publishing Careers;* and *Trade Book Marketing: A Practical Guide,* of which he was general editor. He is also the author of two mystery novels, *Casual Slaughters* and *Final Edit,* both published by Mysterious Press/Warner Books.

S. William Pattis founded and served as Chairman/CEO of NTC Publishing Group from 1961 until 1996, when the firm was acquired by Tribune Company (NYSE). NTC published more than four thousand titles under various imprints including Passport Books, National Textbook, NTC Business Books, VGM Career Books, Teach Yourself, and The Quilt Digest Press. Pattis also served as Chairman/CEO of 3M/Pattis, an advertising sales firm he founded in 1959 and operated as The Pattis Group. In 1988 the business was acquired by the Advertising Services Group of the 3M Company (NYSE).

In addition, for more than two decades, Pattis served as President and Director of P-B Communications, publisher of Chicago's *NORTH SHORE Magazine,* which was purchased by Hollinger International (NYSE) in 1997. In September

1996 Pattis opened a family-investment office, Next Chapter Holdings, L.P., in Highland Park, Illinois, and that is currently the focus of his business activities.

His other business experiences include twenty-five years of service as Director of the Bank of Highwood in Highwood, Illinois, and twelve years as Director of the new Century Bank in Mundelein, Illinois. He is a past member of the Executive Committee of the Publishing Hall of Fame and has maintained active interest in real estate in Illinois, California, and Texas. Since 1989 he has served as Trustee of Eisenhower Medical Center in Rancho Mirage, California, and is a member of the Eisenhower Executive Committee. In addition he is a Director and for four years served as Vice Chairman of the Annenberg Center for the Health Sciences, also in Rancho Mirage. From 1996 through 1999 he served on the Board of the Fund for America's Libraries for the American Library Association. His current activities include involvement as a Director of the Israeli/American Internet firm, Versaware, Inc., and as Vice Chairman of the Stanford, Connecticut, publishing firm, Educational Media LLC.

During the period of 1986–1992, he served the U.S. government as Chairman of the Book & Library Advisory Committee of the United States Information Agency. He is a former member of the U.S. Department of Commerce Industry Sector Advisory Committee for Consumer Goods. In 1992 Pattis was honored with an appointment from President George Bush to the National Security Education Board of the Department of Defense.

In 1968 Bill Pattis received a commendation from Vice President Hubert H. Humphrey and again in 1970 from Vice President Spiro Agnew for his work on the President's Council for Youth Opportunity. In 1988 Bill Pattis joined Charles Z. Wick, Director of the U.S. Information Agency, and participated in the first U.S.–U.S.S.R. Bilateral Information Talks in Moscow, involving leaders from American media and Soviet counterparts. As a result of this work, he was named Chairman of the American Delegation for print media in follow-up talks with the Soviets in February 1990 in Washington, DC, and again in November in Moscow.

He is a former Trustee of the American Council of Teachers of Russian and has served as Trustee on the boards of the Photography for Youth Foundation, Directories International, and the Institute for Human Creativity. In 1971 Pattis received the Humanitarian Man-of-the-Year Award from the American Jewish Committee for his work with inner city youth. Pattis has authored five career books on media for young people including, *Opportunities in Advertising* (1995); *Opportunities in Publishing Careers* (1995), and *Careers in Advertising* (1996). Additional writings have appeared in media and publishing journals. His speaking engagements include appearances before The National Association of

Publishers Representatives, The Overseas Press and Media Association, and the Medill School of Journalism at Northwestern University.

In 1986, under the sponsorship of the U.S. Information Agency, he conducted seminars for Chinese educators in Beijing, China, in the teaching of American English. He was a key speaker at the first Face-to-Face International Publishing Conference in The Hague, Netherlands, and was a principal speaker at the annual meeting of the Periodical Publishers Association of the United Kingdom.

In the spring of 1992 Pattis received the Senator Paul Simon Award, which is given annually to the person who has made the greatest contribution to the field of international studies and foreign language education. In 1997 he was the recipient of the Distinguished Service Award, which is awarded annually within the book publishing industry.

He is married to the former Bette Z. Levin of Los Angeles and has two married children, Mark R. Pattis of Highland Park, Illinois, and Robin Q.P. Himovitz of Montecito, California, and five grandchildren. Bill Pattis is a resident of Highland Park, Illinois, and is a winter resident of Rancho Mirage, California.

This edition has been thoroughly revised by Blythe Camenson, a full-time writer of career books. Camenson's main concern is helping job seekers make educated choices. She firmly believes that with enough information, readers can find long-term, satisfying careers.

Camenson's interests range from history and photography to writing novels. She is also director of Fiction Writer's Connection, a membership organization whose function is to help new writers improve their craft and learn the ropes to getting published. Her website can be found at www.fictionwriters.com.

Camenson has more than three dozen books in print, most published by NTC/Contemporary Books. She is also the coauthor of *Your Novel Proposal: From Creation to Contract* (Writer's Digest Books, 1999). Upcoming titles include *Careers in Writing* and *Careers in Publishing*.

She was educated in Boston, earning her B.A. in English and psychology from the University of Massachusetts and her M.Ed. in counseling from Northeastern University.

FOREWORD

Publishing! I fell in love with books at an early age, but never dreamt I would spend my life in the publishing business. Like so many people with varied interests and a liberal arts education, I ended up in publishing by accident. How, I wondered, could all these varied interests be useful? They are all useful in the book business, and twenty-five years later I still find my work challenging and interesting.

And just what, I've often been asked, is the publishing business? For some, it's the experience of retail, whether in an independent bookstore or as part of one of the chains. Retail bookselling puts you at the crux of the publishing business—the place where all the work of writer and publisher meets the reader.

For others it is work in a publishing house, where there are many opportunities: editorial, design, publicity, marketing, or sales. There are few large publishers, primarily in New York, and many independent publishers located throughout the country. All product quality books, and the working atmosphere is as varied as the books each publishes. Yet another group (one to which I now belong) who feeds the publishers is that of literary agents, who look for new writing talent and new ideas for books and make the connections between writer and publisher.

All of us in the book business share a love of books and find kindred spirits among our colleagues. As a group, publishing people tend to be independent and creative thinkers, intellectually curious, quirky, savvy, and interesting. Be they editorial assistants or top executives, they are almost always congenial.

The publishing world—from writer to publisher to bookstore—has an aura that's difficult to explain but palpable to anyone in the business. Although it is a business and is concerned with profit, it generally does not attract anyone whose primary goal is making money. Rather, the attraction is to be a participant in the process of creating and marketing books. There are opportunities to make a good living in the publishing business, but an underpaid apprenticeship is often required.

One of the best things about publishing is its unpredictability. This is, of course, one of the most frustrating things as well. The public reaction—or lack thereof—to books is often surprising and provides us all with continual challenges.

In the end, though, for me it's about love of books, ideas, and writing. I love the feeling of being in a room (or warehouse or store) full of books. I love the thrill of discovering a new writer. I love seeing a finished book in my hands—a book that came to me as an idea from a writer. I love introducing readers to new writers. I love talking with others who are doing the same thing. I have a sense of mission about my work and know that many others do, too.

Although many who begin a career in publishing spend their lives in it, others do not. In any case, if you are not sure what you want to do in life and are attracted to the publishing industry, give it a try. Whether it becomes your lifelong passion or is merely a way station to another career, you will find it stimulating.

Linda Roghaar
Linda Roghaar Literary Agency, Inc.
Amherst, MA

INTRODUCTION

THE HISTORY OF BOOK PUBLISHING

"**pub.lish** *v.* To bring to the public attention; to announce. From Latin *publicare,* to make public."—*The American Heritage Dictionary of the English Language.*

Publishing is described in the *Encyclopedia Britannica* as "the activity that involves selection, preparation, and marketing of printed matter. It has grown from small and ancient beginnings into a vast and complex industry responsible for the dissemination of all kinds of cultural material, from the most elevated to the most trivial. Its impact upon civilization is impossible to calculate."

To begin with, books, in one form or another, have been around for 4,000 to 5,000 years. Papyrus rolls were used in Egypt as early as the year 3,000 B.C. The first modern form of the book was the Roman *codex,* in which sheets of papyrus were folded vertically to make leaves.

The idea of the newspaper, too, is as old as ancient Rome, where the events of each day were published in a scroll called the *Acta Diurna,* roughly "the acts of the day." Started around 59 B.C., it was the first newspaper of any kind.

As for magazines, they appeared much later on the scene. Though there may have been approaches to a magazine in antiquity, especially in China, the magazine as it is now known began only after the invention of the printing press in the West. The word *magazine* comes to us from France, where one of the world's first magazines, called *Journal des Scavans,* was first published in Paris in 1655.

The history of publishing in its various forms—book, newspaper, and magazine—is characterized by the interplay of technical innovation and social change. Publishing as it is known today is dependent on three major inventions—writing, paper, and printing—and one crucial social development—the spread of literacy.

Before the invention of writing, information could only be exchanged by word of mouth, with all its limitations of time and space. Writing originally was confined to the recording of codes of law, genealogies, and religious formulations. Not until the monopoly of letters, usually held by a priestly caste, was broken could writing finally be used to disseminate information.

The Chinese are generally considered to have invented printing in the sixth century A.D. in the form of wooden block printing. The fifteenth century witnessed the two most important developments in the history of publishing: paper, which the Chinese had invented in 105 A.D. and which the Arabs brought to Europe; and the invention of movable type, generally attributed to Johannes Gutenberg.

Book publishing, the senior member of this triumvirate, began in the United States in 1638, when the first printers, Stephen Daye and his two sons, went from Cambridge, England, to Cambridge, Massachusetts. There they produced their first book, *The Whole Booke of Psalmes,* in 1640. It is known today as "The Bay Psalm Book"—and is understandably rare. The first newspaper in America appeared fifty years later, with the issuing of *Publick Occurrences Both Foreign and Domestick* in 1690, the work of a recently arrived English printer named Benjamin Harris. Fifty-one years after that, on February 16, 1741, came the first American magazine, appropriately named *American Magazine,* or *A Monthly View of the Political State of the British Colonies,* published by the Philadelphia printer Andrew Bradford. A few days later *The General Magazine, and Historical Chronicle, for All the British Plantations in America* appeared, published by a fellow Philadelphian and rival printer, Benjamin Franklin.

There was a good reason for the delay of the magazine. Books and newspapers came first because they were necessities as the colonies established themselves. Magazines had to wait until the literary and practical arts had developed enough in America to create an audience large enough for its own periodicals.

In the eighteenth century, American book production was substantial; in the nineteenth, it burgeoned, with some eight million titles published. A number of important technological developments, in the book trade as in other industries, dramatically raised output and lowered costs. Stereotyping, the iron press, the application of steam power, mechanical typesetting—these inventions amounted to a revolution in book production. A thirst for improvement and entertainment greatly expanded readership, leading to a rapid increase in every category of book from self-help to romantic novels. At this time, publishing assumed its characteristic blend of idealism and commerce.

Bestsellers appeared early along. The first of them was *Charlotte Temple,* a tear-jerking romantic novel about a girl seduced and abandoned by a British army officer. Written by Hannah Rawson and first published in 1797, the book went into two hundred printings. In the eighteenth century, Harriet Beecher Stowe's *Uncle Tom's Cabin* was a runaway bestseller here and in England and is given some credit, rightly or wrongly, for helping to precipitate our Civil War.

Newspapers in the colonial period were largely propaganda machines, spreading protest and eventual independence from Britain on the one hand and the views of Tory sympathizers on the other. The eighteenth century, however, saw the growth of a maturing American newspaper industry, fed by the First Amendment to the Constitution guaranteeing freedom of speech and the press. To appreciate fully what this freedom meant after the repression and censorship of colonial America, it is necessary to remember that the press that was being protected bore little resemblance to the one we know today. It was operating in a period often called the Dark Ages of Journalism, because newspapers had fallen into the hands of the rival political parties, the Federalists of George Washington and Alexander Hamilton, and the Anti-Federalists (later the Democrats) of Thomas Jefferson. No attempt was made to report news objectively, and the papers themselves were used by politicians to attack the other side, often in terms so vicious that they would make today's political editorials or columns seem mild and inoffensive. Men like Washington and Jefferson were accused of the most heinous crimes by the opposition papers.

The early nineteenth century saw the revolutionizing of the newspaper business by a single individual, James Gordon Bennett Sr., a tall, slim, eccentric Scotsman who had come to America penniless, worked on several papers from Boston to Savannah, and at last borrowed $500 and started his own *New York Herald,* doing all the reporting himself and printing it in a Wall Street basement on an old press with battered type. Bennett and his *Herald* transformed newspapering by showing America and the world how to get the news. He organized a city room in much the same way it is today, established foreign correspondents, set up the first Washington bureau, and employed the newly invented telegraph to get the news first from everywhere the lines reached. Now the news—not politics—ranked first in importance. Bennett did not hesitate to be political, but he did it primarily on his editorial page.

Six years after the *Herald* appeared, Horace Greeley started the *New York Tribune.* Greeley was followed in 1851 by Henry J. Raymond, who founded the *New York Times,* with its slogan "All the news that's fit to print."

Following the Civil War, the newspaper business boomed as never before. The Gilded Age, as the period was known, produced such newspaper giants as rival publishers Joseph Pulitzer, with his *New York World,* and William Randolph Hearst, founder of the *San Francisco Examiner* and the *New York Journal.* It is Hearst who generally is credited with starting the Spanish-American War in 1898 by his coverage of events in Cuba, though Pulitzer also clamored for war.

Hearst's brand of newspaper coverage was known as "yellow journalism," from Outcault's Yellow Kid, whose costume was printed in yellow ink, the first use of color in a newspaper. The phrase came to mean sensational journalism of any kind.

As for the magazine publishing business, its turning point came in 1825, a year of ferment and change at home and abroad. In Europe, a tide of revolution and reform was running; at home, a grassroots revolt had placed a Populist president from the West, Andrew Jackson, in the White House, and a new consciousness of their country as a nation had gripped Americans. Education was spreading rapidly, the illiteracy rate was falling, and the cities were mushrooming. Daily newspapers with circulations of more than one hundred thousand soon arose. Mass-audience paperbacks appeared for the first time in 1842, and for magazines, the result was a great outpouring of publications of every conceivable kind, reaching out to meet the needs of the new, large audiences created by growth and change.

The golden age for magazines came in the quarter-century from 1825 to 1850, when the business as we know it today really began. In 1825 there were fewer than a hundred magazines in America; by 1850 there were more than six hundred, the survivors of between four and five thousand periodicals issued in that quarter-century. Three magazines founded during this period are still surviving: *Scientific American,* begun in 1845, and *Harper's Magazine,* founded in 1850 as *Harper's New Monthly Magazine.* Its rival was and remains the *Atlantic Monthly,* established in 1857.

In the twentieth century, all three forms of publishing thrived and today are among the wonders of modern American life. Most of today's prominent book publishing houses were started in this century, from McGraw-Hill (1909), Alfred A. Knopf (1915), Simon & Schuster (1924), Random House and Viking (1925), to such later entries in the field as Crown (1936) and Atheneum (1959). The advent of the contemporary mass-market paperback in 1939 with Pocket Books was followed by houses such as Avon (1941) and Bantam Books (1946), among others, which came into existence to supply America's apparently insatiable demand for inexpensive and portable books. Magazine publishers such as American Heritage and Time-Life opened mail-order book divisions in the early 1960s. In recent years, the explosive growth of small presses, perhaps fifteen thousand or more altogether as of 1994, some publishing only one or two titles, must be noted. The last decades of the century also have seen the merging of many once individually owned firms or their purchase by major corporations—a trend not without its detractors who fear the concentration of power in a few hands.

In the newspaper field, this century has witnessed an increased objectivity of press coverage, largely due to the importance of advertising revenue over circulation; newspapers today are business institutions, increasingly run by business owners, and no longer the tools of a political party or an individual entrepreneur. Tabloids also appeared in the 1920s, beginning with the *New York Daily News*. With the threat to advertising lineage posed by competition from television, the press has become much more diversified. Newspapers today are likely to be parts of a chain under single ownership, such as the Gannett chain of more than one hundred papers, most prominently *USA Today*. The second primary change worth noting is the rise of syndication, allowing even small-town newspapers to have editorial material, information, and entertainment features they could not otherwise afford to publish. Newspapers are still changing, but this change is now primarily due to new technology, as we shall see in later chapters.

Highlights of the twentieth century in the magazine business include the rise (and fall) of such mass-circulation periodicals as *The Saturday Evening Post, Collier's, Liberty,* and *Life*. Success stories were written by the *Reader's Digest,* founded in October 1921 by De Witt and Lila Bell Wallace with an investment of $5,000; *Time,* started on a shoestring in 1923 by Henry Luce and his partner Briton Hadden; and *The New Yorker,* the creation of editor Harold Ross in 1925. The so-called "little" magazines proliferated in the 1920s, introducing such important writers as Ernest Hemingway. The literary journals, more numerous than ever today, still serve the same function.

Since World War II several trends have emerged in the magazine business. There has been a continuing and decided trend toward special-interest publications because it has become difficult to edit a magazine for more than a relatively small part of our population. There is also a trend towards regional, city, and even demographic editions of national magazines in an effort to reach specific segments of an audience. Finally, there has been growth in the number of magazines with "controlled" circulation, meaning that they are sent free to members of a specific audience. For example, the nation's largest-circulation magazine, *Modern Maturity,* is sent to members of the American Association of Retired Persons (AARP).

In this book, we shall examine each aspect of publishing in turn and the career opportunities each presents. By the time you finish this book, we, the co-authors, are confident you will know which part of the many-faceted publishing business is for you—and you for it—and you will also know how to go about becoming a part of the fascinating publishing scene.

Robert A. Carter
S. William Pattis

PART ONE

BOOK PUBLISHING

CHAPTER 1

TODAY'S BOOK PUBLISHING INDUSTRY

More than 60,000 books will be published in North America this year. That's more than 160 books a day! We'll spend about $20 billion buying those books. Book publishing is big business.

Who publishes all these books? Eight media conglomerates, along with perhaps a dozen of the largest independent publishers, corner between 75 and 85 percent of the market.

The eight megacorporations that dominate book publishing in North America are (with some of their major publishing imprints in parentheses):

1. Hearst Corporation (Avon, William Morrow)
2. News Corporation/Rupert Murdock (HarperCollins)
3. Pearson PLC (Penguin, G.P. Putnam, Berkley)
4. Viacom (Simon & Schuster, Pocket Books)
5. Advance/Newhouse (Random House, Knopf, Modern Library, Ballentine)
6. Bertelsmann AG (Bantam, Doubleday, Dell, Dial)
7. Time Warner/Ted Turner (Little Brown, Book of the Month)
8. Holtzbrinck (Farrar, Straus & Giroux, St. Martin's Press, Henry Holt)

After the "Big Eight," another 2,200 publishers do enough business each year to qualify for listing by the U.S. Commerce Bureau. *Literary Market Place,* the industry reference published by R.R. Bowker, lists another 18,000 to 20,000 smaller and independent publishers.

PUBLISHING'S ALLIED GROUPS

Although people use the words *book industry, book business,* and *book trade* interchangeably, the latter phrase is more specifically employed to describe retail booksellers. As a business, or industry, publishing is made up of eight closely allied groups.

1. Literary Agencies. First come the literary agencies. They are the primary channel through which book manuscripts get to publishers for general bookstore *sale–trade books* as they are known. Other kinds of books do not often come through agents, and only a small percentage of trade books are not agented. If a publisher had about five thousand manuscripts submitted annually—and that would be average for a medium-sized house—most would be unsolicited and unagented. Working in a literary agency, or even starting one, is a career opportunity people seldom think of. You can read more about entering this field in Chapter 4.

2. Publishers. The publishers themselves, along with their various departments, comprise the second group, and the jobs they offer are described at length in this Chapters 1 and 4.

3. Book Manufacturers. A third group consists of the people who make books—the manufacturers. They include compositors, engravers, printers, binders, and similar technicians who are not necessarily involved exclusively in bookmaking. Manufacturers have to be supplied, and that means the people who make type, ink, paper, binding material, and the other ingredients of book manufacture must be included in this group. Read more about book manufacturing in Chapter 4.

4. Book Reviewers and Critics. A fourth category in the industry includes book reviewers and critics, who are some of the links between publishing and the public. The distinction between reviewers and critics is that the reviewers, while their writing is critical, are really reporting on books in daily, weekly, or monthly media, while the critics are essentially literary essayists who may use one book or several books as the basis for their commentaries. The *New York Times Book Review,* the *Washington Post Book World,* and the *Chicago Tribune Book World* are the chief reviewing media among the newspapers, but many of the nation's other major newspapers also have daily or Sunday book sections with reviews written by staff writers or freelancers. Some use syndicated book review columns. Magazines such as *Harper's, The Atlantic Monthly,* and *The New Yorker,* among others, do both critical writing and reviewing, while purely literary criticism is found chiefly in the *New York Review of Books* and in magazines such as *Commentary, The American Scholar,* and *Partisan Review.* Creating a career for yourself as a book reviewer is covered in Chapter 13.

5. Advertising Agencies/Related Services. The fifth group consists of advertising agencies and related services, which are designed to sell books. There is a long list of advertising agencies serving the industry in varying degrees, and to these would have to be added another list of consulting and editorial services, marketing and sales departments in book publish-

ing houses, public relations organizations, research groups, direct mail specialists, and compilers of mailing lists. Careers in this area are covered in Chapter 4.

6. Warehouses. Sixth is the group that services warehouses, where books are stored before they go out to retailers and wholesalers—the link between the publishers and the bookstores, libraries, schools and colleges, and others who are buyers of books.

7. Selling Outlets. The retails stores themselves and the book departments in other stores comprise the seventh category, and it is a large one, with thousands of outlets of every kind. Retail bookstores and chain stores (*the trade*) are the backbone of this group, but many department stores have active book divisions, and there are steadily increasing sales through drug and stationery stores, supermarkets, airport kiosks, and other kinds of nonbook retail outlets. Important concerns to add to the list include Internet outlets such as Amazon.com and Barnes and Noble and scores of other specialty retailers, who stock from just a handful of titles to every book available on the market.

8. "Reprinters." Finally, in the eighth category are the people who buy, sometimes for extremely high figures, the right to republish material from books in other forms—book clubs, reprint houses, magazines, newspaper syndicates, filmmakers, and broadcasters.

Libraries

Libraries are not actually part of the publishing industry, but they can hardly be left out of what constitutes it. With their own five divisions—public, private, school, college, and special—they offer a substantial market in themselves, to which most publishers pay special attention.

These, then, are the overall dimensions of the book business. Now let's take a look at the major types of publishing the industry has to offer, each of which is described in detail later in this chapter.

AN OVERVIEW OF TYPES OF PUBLISHERS

Trade Book Publishing. Trade books are titles designed for the general consumer and are sold through retail and discount outlets and to public and specialized libraries. They may be hardcover or paperbound, for adults or for young readers.

A certain confusion comes with the word *trade,* which in the book business also is used to designate the retail market or *"trade."* A *trade publication* refers to a periodical published for a specific business or occupation. *Publisher's Weekly* is the trade journal of the book publishing industry, for example.

Regional/Small Presses. Regional and small presses mainly cater to specialty and special interest markets. Each publishing house has carved its own niche with its own signature and may produce fiction or nonfiction or both. As an example, you'd more likely find a New Orleans or Santa Fe travel guide published locally, than by any of the "Big Eight."

Religion Publishing. Religion books include bibles, testaments, prayer books and missals, and hymnals. Sunday school materials are not included, but religion publishers and the religion departments of general trade houses also publish inspirational books, works on theology, and even titles dealing with social problems. In addition, the religion market includes a large component of fiction, with novels highlighting different religious themes.

Textbook Publishing. Textbook publishing is divided into two categories: elementary and secondary school textbooks (known as "el-hi" texts) and college textbooks.

Technical, Scientific, Special Interest, and Medical Publishing. This area covers what we loosely call *professional books,* because their market is the people who work in these various careers: businesspeople, managers, accountants, lawyers, computer specialists, physicians, nurses, hospital administrators, engineers, architects, etc. For virtually every profession, there is a body of literature.

University Presses. For the most part, these are nonprofit departments of universities, colleges, museums, or other research organizations, publishing books primarily of scholarly or regional interest, though university presses on occasion bring out books of interest to the general public (and even a bestseller now and then).

Organizational/Sponsored Presses. Many organizations have their own publishing arms, and some will sponsor or subsidize projects of special merit and interest to their employees, stockholders, or other interested parties. Every once in a while, a book issued by an organizational press breaks through and finds a national market. Tom Clancy's first publisher for *The Hunt for Red October* was the Naval Institute Press, which nearly sank trying to keep up with the demand.

Paperback Publishing. Paperback publishing includes both mass-market paperbacks—which are distinguished by their size (they are all the same rack size, approximately $4\frac{7}{8}$ by 7 inches) and their mode of distribution through newsstands, chain stores, drugstores, supermarkets, convenience stores, airports, and other outlets where magazines are sold—and trade paperbacks, which may be any size at all and are sold for the most part through retail bookstores.

Mail-Order Publishing and Book Clubs. Although book clubs seldom create their own publications they have traditionally been considered a part of the book industry, rather than as channels of distribution. Mail-order publishers, on the other hand, do create their own publications, and market them, as the name implies, through direct-mail solicitation and coupon advertising. The book clubs, too, market their selections by mail-order and newspaper and magazine advertising.

Book Packagers/Producers. This relatively new breed of publishing is growing rapidly. A book packager or producer acts as an intermediary, selling a concept to a publisher and then contracting with the author to create the book.

Subsidy and Cooperative Publishing. There is a definite distinction to these two forms of publishing. Subsidy publishers (also known as vanity presses) often work with writers who are unable to find a traditional publisher for their work. The writer covers all of the cost of publication, publicity, and distribution. Cooperative publishers ask writers to participate in the cost of production. Many small publishers work in all three categories, publishing some books on a commercial basis, some with a co-op deal, and still others on full author subsidy.

Electronic Publishing. There's a lot of publishing activity online these days—and a lot of controversy surrounding it. Will it last, or is it just a fad? Online publishers offer consumers alternative and economical avenues compatible with our high-tech lifestyles.

U.S. Government. The United States Government, through its Printing Office is, undoubtedly, the largest publisher of all, accounting for thousands of titles a year.

Although the above is a comprehensive overview of the diverse forms of the publishing business as a whole, they are far from the end of its variety. A substantial group of publishers, for example, operate the book divisions of religious organizations, and other groups perform the same type of services for professional and technical associations. Nor should we overlook the more than fifteen thousand university theses published annually.

TRADE BOOK PUBLISHING

Adult Books

We have already defined a "trade" book as one designed to be sold through the retail trade and to libraries. Admittedly, that definition does not clarify the matter much. How about, books for the general reader? That's somewhat better. Rather than describing trade books by their channels of distribution, we might be closer to the mark if we relate them to their consumers, the readers—in other words, you and me. Trade books are the books we most frequently buy for entertainment, information, or to aid in the pursuit of a particular hobby or pastime. They are the books we are free to choose for ourselves—not assigned to us, like textbooks.

Their variety is infinite. First, there is *fiction.* The invention of the English popular novel is generally credited to a writer named Thomas Deloney, a writer of ballads, pamphlets, and prose stories who lived in the last decades of the sixteenth century. The form has been going strong ever since. Although the death knell for the novel is frequently sounded by jaded critics, fiction continues to be popular. According to industry figures some nine thousand titles were published in a recent year under the category of "fiction," which surely indicated no slackening in demand. Most of these, however, are not what we would describe as "literature." In the fiction category are mysteries, westerns, gothic novels, novels of horror and the occult, and scads of romance—romances of all kinds, from first love for teenagers to X-rated heavy-breathers. There's also science fiction, fantasy, action/adventure, historical novels and thrillers—legal thrillers, medical thrillers, techno-thrillers. Short stories, too, continue to be collected and read.

After fiction there is, well *nonfiction,* whose definition is equally as broad. Samuel S. Vaughan, a distinguished editor and publisher, asks:

> What is nonfiction, after all? It includes poetry, which at its best is truth, but it is not limited to the factual. It includes biography, history, belles lettres, religion, instruction, sciences (soft, social, hard, practical, theoretical). It includes, in short, everything that the word "fiction" does not. It is, in other words, "everything else." Thus nonfiction is…inept, inappropriate, inelegant…a nondescript description.

Books on the following should also be included on this list of "everything else": reference, dictionaries, travel, and business.

Critics frequently cite overproduction of titles as one of the industry's most serious problems. "Too many books!" the cry goes up. But who can say what is too many and what is enough? And who will be the first to cut production? Will it be the author who will sacrifice her or his brainchild? The publisher, with a balanced list in mind? What seems to work best is the ruthlessness of the marketplace itself. If a book is selling, for whatever reason, it will most likely remain in print and available, until it stops selling.

For that matter, most publishers realize that most of their titles are ephemeral, even if bound in durable covers and printed on acid-free paper good for several centuries. Most books are meant to "strut and fret their brief hour upon the stage, and then be heard no more," as Shakespeare put it. That is not to say that they are not worth writing or not worth publishing; merely that they do not have staying power. They do not join a publisher's *backlist,* titles that go on selling year after year, often for decades. Such books include *Bartlett's Quotations,* first published in 1855 and continuously in print, in various revisions, ever since; *The Fannie Farmer Cookbook,* first issued in 1906; and *Gone With the Wind,* which celebrated its fiftieth anniversary in 1986 and still sells some one hundred thousand copies a year in various editions.

Children's Books

In spite of television and the other distractions of life today—video and computer games and videocassette recorders, sports, and other leisure-time activities—children are still book readers, as the circulation figures of school and public libraries show. Young children want to be read to, older ones quickly move into all kinds of reading, and by time they are twelve, a good many of them are reading adult books.

Consequently, the task of the children's book editor and her or his staff covers a broad area, and it is far from an easy job in a competitive and rapidly changing market.

In some publishing houses children's books are referred to as "juveniles," a term their editors find offensive. As one irritated editor pointed out: "Would you call adult books 'seniles'?" Whatever they are called—children's books or "books for young readers," they usually fall into three different classifications: *picture books* for preschoolers and ages five through seven, *middle-age books* for ages eight through twelve, and *young adult* or *YA* titles for teenagers.

Since so many books for children depend to a great extent on illustration, this is a field where artists and experts in graphics have a virtually unlimited opportunity to exercise their creativity. Consequently, people in the children's book department should know something about both graphics and art, and those who come to it with at least some background in these fields will be more valuable.

The children's book department is a publishing house in miniature: it has editors, copyeditors, proofreaders, production and design people, and publicity, promotion, advertising, and sales personnel. As the children's book business has expanded, the autonomous department has slowly given way except for the small houses, where three or four people do all the work, and the largest ones, which have the "house-in-miniature" structure just described. In between, these days, is something both new and old, a nineteenth-century organization revived by necessity. Here the editorial work is done by the children's book department, from choosing manuscripts to exercising general supervision, but all the other functions (copyediting, promotion, sales, etc.) are carried out by the departments that handle them for the entire house. When this is the case, there are varying degrees of relationship between the children's book department and these other units, depending on the house.

REGIONAL/SMALL PRESSES

While the "Big Eight" have sewn up New York, thousands of regional publishers and small presses are thriving throughout the rest of North America. Most never see their books covered in the *New York Times Book Review*—much less make the bestseller list—but some do.

Small presses can afford to take chances that the big guys wouldn't, because they can survive on considerably smaller sales than their more cumbersome and better known colleagues.

They are often superb at servicing specialty and special interest markets and specific regions of the country. If you are looking for a novel about a female veteran, who is left-handed and a Scorpio, trying to find love in the mountains of Colorado, you might just find a small press specializing in books featuring left-handed, female, veteran Scorpios set in Colorado.

Many small presses are established and operated by writers and/or editors who are disillusioned with the offerings on the bestseller lists and are dedicated to publishing outstanding fiction and nonfiction.

There's no such thing as a typical small press, but you would expect to find that the small press publishes fewer titles than the big publishers (as few as one per year), has smaller press runs for the first edition (two thousand to five thousand copies), and offers small or nonexistent advances for its writers.

Many small presses lack the firepower to get national distribution and the kind of push needed to generate big sales. However, lots of small presses look for breakout books to take them national.

To find regional publishers and small presses, look in your library for Len Fulton's *The International Directory of Little Magazines and Small Presses,* the source for independent publishers. Fulton also produces a monthly magazine reviewing small press publishers. Contact: Dustbooks, Box 100, Paradise, California 95967.

RELIGION PUBLISHING

According to the *Encyclopedia Britannica,* "the contents of the earliest books, whatever their origin, are almost always religious or semireligious—hymns, prayers, and rites that put man in touch with the divine, and myths, legends, and epics that give an account of his origins." Certainly this was true of the first

American colonists. Not only was the first published book in this country a collection of psalms, as we have noted, but the libraries of the colonists were heavily religious in nature, and every household, whether there was a library or not, had its family Bible.

Religion book publishing was the staple of the trade at the very outset. These books came not only from the presses of printers who were issuing general lists, but also from the churches, which established their own publishing houses very early. The Methodist Publishing House, for example, was founded in 1789, and the Baptists were not far behind. Today nearly every Protestant denomination is represented, and the Catholics have many outlets—from organizations within the church like the Paulist Press, to such religious trade houses as Ave Maria Press, Morehouse-Barlow Inc., and Orbis Books. *Literary Market Place* lists 147 Catholic, 63 Buddhist, 46 Hindu, 50 Islamic, 110 Jewish, 199 Protestant, and 242 "other" religion book publishers.

Several of the large general publishing houses—including HarperCollins, Doubleday, Holt, Rinehart & Winston, and Macmillan—have religion book departments. Other houses, such as McGraw-Hill, have religion book editors on staff.

Religion publishing, then, can be controlled by the churches, be a department of a regular publishing house, or be completely independent. Whatever form it takes—bibles, hymnals, prayer books, novels, or inspirational books—its basic components are the same as in other kinds of publishing: editorial, production, advertising, and sales.

TEXTBOOK PUBLISHING

Textbook publishing is only one area of specialization within the larger field of educational publishing—what has come to be called the *educational materials business*. This terms denotes a recognition of the fact that in our time, education by the printed word has been supplemented (and in a few cases even replaced) by audiovisual devices, from teaching machines to films and recordings. The publishing of textbooks alone, however, on all levels, accounts for about one third of the total annual income from book publishing. Performing a basic service to education, it serves as a preparation for all other areas of book publishing, inasmuch as it is largely responsible for creating a reading public in the first place.

As in most other kinds of specialized publishing, textbooks and other educational materials can be produced by a department in a general publishing house or by a separate specialized enterprise. There are several large textbook houses and many smaller ones that specialize within the specialty. Like religion books, textbook publishing has its roots in the beginnings of the book business, since religion and education were among the first concerns of the colonists.

Textbook publishing begins at the elementary and high school levels, commonly abbreviated in the trade as "el-hi." A company or department may specialize in this area alone, or it may also publish college texts, or confine itself to the colleges. In whatever field or fields it chooses to operate, a house also may acquire a reputation for a particular kind of book. One house in the el-hi business, for example, has been known for nearly a century as the leader in supplying texts for music education, although it publishes in other subjects as well.

The output of these houses is divided into hardback and paperback textbooks, teachers' editions, workbooks, standard tests, and miscellaneous manuals for grades one through eight. A similar array is published for high schools and still another for colleges. Most of these producers are exclusively textbook houses, as opposed to departments in general houses, and most are el-hi publishers. When they are departments, their list is usually in the college field.

A difference between text and trade is the textbook publisher's need to maintain a large inventory. The trade house markets what it can of a title within a year and sells whatever remains to a discount firm—a process called *remaindering*. But the textbook publisher has sales of a title spread over a period of years, and that may be the case with most of the titles. As a result, the textbook publisher's inventory is often twice as large as that of an ordinary business, and the margin of profit is substantially smaller.

TECHNICAL, SCIENTIFIC, SPECIAL INTEREST, AND MEDICAL PUBLISHING

Though publishing at large tends to think in terms of fiction only, technical, scientific, special interest, and medical publishing comprise another area that is largely unexplored and virtually unknown to most people who seek careers in publishing. Many of its practices are like those of the trade book field, but others relate closer to textbook publishing. Technical and scientific books, for example, are generally written for a professional audience, but others are sold to a much larger public. Special-interest books covering the areas of business, art, travel, reference, computers, gardening, cookery, self-help, golf, photography, outdoor living, and so forth, are in demand by amateurs and professionals alike and are at the heart of the publishing industry. Most medical books are meant for doctors, but in psychology and psychiatry, thousands of titles are read by nonprofessionals.

Although it is difficult to define exactly, technical book publishing is generally considered to embrace five fields: the mechanical arts; mathematics and the natural sciences; engineering and applied sciences, which include agriculture, forestry, military science, medicine, hygiene and public health, psychology, psychiatry, nursing, pharmacy, and dentistry; the social sciences, including anthropology, economics, sociology, and government; and industrial and business administration including computers and electronics. Simply listing these broad fields and remembering that there are so many specializations within each one, opens a vast array of possibilities for job candidates who want to carry their special interests into book publishing. And the list grows longer every year, as new fields develop.

The books that reach this market can also be divided into five general categories. First would come the *manuals.* These are the how-to-do-it books and often reference books, in hard or soft covers, that emphasize organization and clarity. Then there are the *technical textbooks,* sometimes overlapping into the textbook market. They are supplemented by the *theoretical treatises,* both general and specialized, which are intended primarily for graduate students and as reference books for professionals. Another supplemental category includes *monographs,* written by specialists for specialists and covering both theory and application. Finally, there are *handbooks,* which are data compilations intended to help the scientists or engineers in their daily work.

In attempting to make any distinction between a chemistry text and a book about chemistry meant for chemists, there is some overlapping with textbooks. But these distinctions are not confusing to the users of the books and, therefore, are not important.

Like the textbook house, the firm publishing technical books must be well financed. Costs are high because these books are likely to be lengthy and crammed with diagrams, charts, tables, and similar paraphernalia that make for expensive composition. Everything that goes into the making of such books—illustrations, paper, binding, printing, and editorial work—must be of the highest quality, which adds to the expense. It costs anywhere form two to ten times more to produce a technical book than a trade book of comparable size. The technical book costs much more, but it sells at a far slower pace, over a longer period of time, and it may be years before it begins to make money for the publisher.

Even the smallest technical book may require a minimum investment of $25,000 or more, while large and complicated works represent an investment in the hundreds of thousands of dollars. The only compensation is that the technical book publisher takes fewer risks than the trade house, since technical publishers, like textbook publishers, have the ability to calculate the market carefully. They know, for example, the precise number of microbiologists who would be interested in a new handbook in the field and precisely how many college courses are taught in the subject; from this they can determine the "universe," or total size, of their market.

Nevertheless, the technical publisher's business must be well capitalized, because it is a long time between the concept of a new technical book and the day it begins to earn money. Competition for technical experts who can write is vigorous, and after the contract is signed, it may be a long time before the publisher receives the finished manuscript. It takes anywhere from two to ten years to prepare a technical manuscript, even longer in the case of some technical classics.

When the manuscript is delivered, another long period ensues before it can be published. Editing these books is usually a long, laborious process; everything has to be checked and must be correct, or the book's usefulness is sharply diminished. The manufacturing takes longer, too, because the composition is complicated. Consequently it may take as long as two years, and seldom less than six months, for a technical book to go through the production process. This means a large publishing investment tied up for years before returns come in.

Despite the slowness and independence shown by most technical authors, they afford a publisher a distinct advantage over the trade publisher's writers: it is much easier to spot and measure outstanding competence in an engineer or psychiatrist than in a poet, novelist, or biographer. If the technical publisher wants a new book in the field of supercomputers, for example, tracking down several outstanding authorities is fairly easy. Perhaps no more than fifty people in the entire country have the necessary qualifications to do the book. Consulting a few specialists will further narrow the field of choice. Then, to be assured of an authoritative and salable book, the publisher has only to persuade one of the finalists to produce a manuscript. The challenge is to find the right person, and then help that person produce a satisfactory manuscript—which is why the technical editor is so important.

Medical Books

Medical books have to be considered apart from the others. Technically, they belong in the category we have been discussing, but they comprise a small industry in themselves—small because there are relatively few doctors by comparison with the number of scientists and technologists, and, therefore, the market itself is smaller. But there the diminishment ends. Medical books are generally larger than other technical books, cost more to produce, and bear higher prices.

Editors of medical books have a responsibility that does not exist in any other branch of publishing. They are dealing with material that affects human lives; consequently, they have to exercise extreme care at every step. They must be certain, for instance, that the authors they choose to write books are the best authorities available. Accuracy in these books is a vital matter, particularly in descriptions of procedures and medications. This extends to the illustrations, where inaccuracies could lead to faulty interpretations and incorrect diagnoses. If a book is concerned with new discoveries, it cannot be published by a reputable house until the research behind it has been published in the professional journals and accepted generally by specialists in the field.

That heavy responsibility means that people who plan to enter this kind of publishing must not only have a sound background in medicine (even though they need not necessarily be doctors), they must also have the highest ethical and professional standards. Medical publishers are highly conscious of their responsibility. They represent the most conservative part of the publishing industry, and even in a business where ethics are high, they stand out.

A few of the major publishing houses have medical book departments—Little, Brown and McGraw-Hill are perhaps the best known—but most of the books in this field are issued by houses specializing in them, most of which have origins dating back more than a century. Historically, Philadelphia has always been the center of medical publishing, and it remains so today.

UNIVERSITY PRESSES

If the old saying is correct, that a true university is a collection of books, then university presses have helped form the character of our universities. The purpose of these presses, as the publishing divisions of their parent institutions, is to serve scholars and scholarship and to function as conduits of ideas, information, and speculation that help to determine the course of human thought and endeavor.

Although university presses have played an important role in publishing since the late nineteenth century, the general public knows little about them, and even many students are unaware that their universities have one. Their number fluctuates with current economic conditions, but the Association of American University Presses (AAUP)—created as a formal organization in 1937 and established with a central office in New York City since 1959—has at present 105 North American and 5 overseas presses as members. *Literary Market Place* lists 183 university presses, ranging form Ahsahta Press to Yale University Press.

University presses are unique on the publishing scene because they are almost all nonprofit ventures, subsidized for the most part by the universities that house them. There are exceptions to this: Yale University Press, though it has an endowment, receives no operating funds from its parent university and must either pay its own way or depend on grants and outside subsidies. For many years, though, university presses were not intended to make money, and most of them did not. Beginning in the 1970s, financial pressures on higher education forced the presses to take more careful account of their finances; more emphasis was placed on making the presses self-supporting if not profitable, and several of them now do operate at a profit. Some of the smaller presses, unable either to stay in the black by themselves or to get sufficient university support, have banded together and formed regional presses, serving several universities.

University presses began as a means of disseminating the knowledge acquired by their own professors. Doctoral theses became books, and scholarly works whose potential sales were so small that no general publisher would take them on were standard productions of the presses. Eventually, however, a few publishing houses realized that some serious works of scholarship had potentially larger sales, particularly in the fields of history and political science. This realization has spread, and today, university presses are making a solid cultural contribution of books that are read by increasing numbers of literate and concerned people.

For the most part, however, they do not realize large sales. Two or three thousand copies would be an average, although some titles sell more if they concern matters of current general interest in politics or cultural movements. The university presses also have become custodians of our literary heritage, engaged in publishing definitive editions of such great American writers as Mark Twain and Walt Whitman. Some of the presses have been issuing the papers of past presidents and other eminent people. Notable among these volumes are the Harvard University Press's edition of the Adams family papers, which eventually will run to more than a hundred volumes; the Princeton University Press's edition of Thomas Jefferson's papers; and the Yale University Press's papers of Benjamin Franklin.

Other presses are regional and local specialists. The University of Oklahoma Press, for example, is noted for its series of Indian studies, and the University of California Press has published many volumes reflecting different aspects of life in that state—historical, geographical, and cultural.

Except for the fact that the emphasis is on scholarly books, no matter what else may be published, the operation of a university press is much like a commercial press.

They have their special problems, however. The editors of these presses are dealing almost entirely with professors. These men and women are professional experts in their fields and many of them, especially in the humanities, write well, some brilliantly. Since they are, in a sense, academic colleagues, press editors must work cooperatively with them. Most university presses maintain an editorial advisory board, drawn from various disciplines on the faculties, to review manuscripts or outlines so that the prospective authors may be evaluated by their peers.

For the person entering publishing, this small, tightly organized structure offers an excellent learning opportunity. Working on a university press soon makes beginners proficient in most of the skills required in the several departments of a commercial house. Consequently, they are more valuable as employees and have more opportunities open to them if they switch to a general publishing company.

College students who develop an interest in book publishing would do well to consider the press of their university first, if one exists. Sometimes it is possible to get a summer job and begin learning before graduation.

Museum Presses

Other institutional presses also offer job opportunities, especially the presses affiliated with large museums. The Museum of Modern Art and the Metropolitan Museum of Art in New York both have active publishing programs and run their own bookshops. Other museum publishing programs are located in Philadelphia, Baltimore, Los Angeles, and San Francisco. There is also an increasing number of nonprofit cultural institutions all over the United States—perhaps thousands of them, large and small: historical sites and societies, performing arts groups, parks, library service agencies, and other public and quasipublic units—most of which do some form of publishing. Many of them are much too small and too undercapitalized to have trained staffs, but some of them administer energetic and extensive publishing programs of books, catalogs, postcards, prints, and posters.

ORGANIZATIONAL/SPONSORED PRESSES

Some organizations—both for profit and nonprofit—maintain their own publishing departments and sponsor, subsidize, or publish at their own expense books of interest to members, employees, and other related parties. For example, the Adoption Awareness Press, a Division of the Musser Foundation, Cape Coral, Florida, published *Chasing Rainbows: A Search for Family Ties,* about a woman who finds her birth mother about the same time the daughter she had given up for adoption finds her.

As with all publishers, publishing departments sponsored by organizations have the need for publishing personnel, including editors.

PAPERBACK PUBLISHING

Paperbacks are divided into two major categories—*mass market* and *trade*—distinguished from each other both by their formats and by their means of distribution. Mass-market paperbacks are all rack sized, $4\frac{3}{16}$ by $6\frac{7}{8}$ inches, and printed on high-speed rotary presses at two or three plants. They reach the marketplace through national and local distributors who sell them like magazines. Trade paperbacks are sold primarily through the retail book trade, including independent bookstores, chain bookstores, college bookstores, and the book departments of department stores. When first introduced, trade paperbacks were called "quality" paperbacks, and they, too, were rack sized. In the early 1950s, the technology of "perfect" or glued binding had been improved with new machines and adhesives for binding books cheaply. Writes Herbert S. Bailey, Jr., in *The Art and Science of Book Publishing:*

> In 1953 a press at the Doubleday printing plant was underutilized, and Jason Epstein, then a Doubleday editor, only recently a student himself, saw an opportunity to reissue books of intellectual importance at prices that students could afford. He persuaded the officers of Doubleday, and the first series of Anchor Books was issued. The response of the public, and especially of students and professors, showed that an unfulfilled demand had existed, and a new submarket within the larger market for books was created.

This new kind of paperback did not long remain quality oriented, or rack sized either. With the emergence of the counterculture press in the 1960s and early 1970s, a flood of "underground" publications—pamphlets, posters, magazines, and leaflets—poured out of small, independent presses, while mainstream publishers issued everything from esoteric novels to diet and physical fitness books, along with issues-oriented nonfiction, in the trade paper format. Now, of course, trade paperbacks appear in every size and shape, containing every conceivable subject matter. Sometimes they are published simultaneously with hardcover editions, so that reviewers will pay serious attention. Much of the time they are the only edition of a title. As mass-market paperbacks have increased in price, so have trade paperbacks, proportionately; they now sell for what hardcover books sold for twenty-five years ago. All this has led to price resistance to paperbacks; to the book-buying public, they no longer seem quite as affordable as they once were. As for mass-market paperbacks, the days when they were considered cheap are long gone.

Paperback textbooks and *paperback technical books,* third and fourth paperback categories, are sold through the usual educational and technical book channels; the latter are also sold by direct mail. There is considerable overlapping in these categories, however, and often a book can be sold as both a trade and a mass-market product. Paperback categories, publishers, and channels of distribution have become blurred; they are no longer sold in separate, distinct markets.

Marketing Paperbacks

In distributing their products, mass-market paperback publishers often use their own sales representatives or employ national distributors who in turn deal with the local or regional wholesalers. Publishers must use salespeople who know how to sell to the usual trade outlets—bookstores; book departments of department stores; the chains, such as Waldenbooks, Crown, and B. Dalton; superstores like Borders and Barnes & Noble; schools and libraries; the export trade; and more recently, mail order.

Paperback publishers are now aggressively reaching into every market. Education, once closed to them by traditional practice, is becoming a more important source of sales, as financially hard-pressed institutions and students turn to less expensive books. College sales in particular can realize substantial income. Successful titles like *Future Shock* and *The Catcher in the Rye* routinely sell upward of one hundred thousand copies each year, and the mass-market editions of classics such as NAL's Signet Books and Pocket Books's Washington Square editions account for many thousands of copies sold of royalty-free, public-domain titles.

For those thinking of entering book publishing, the paperback field is a fast-paced, exciting place to work. If you think you would enjoy working in a place where every month constitutes a brand-new publishing "season," then you'll probably want to head toward one of the mass market houses.

MAIL-ORDER PUBLISHING AND BOOK CLUBS

Mail-Order Publishing

Americans love to buy things by mail—all sorts of things. Direct marketing accounts for 27 percent of the total U.S. retail dollar sales, according to the Simmons Market Research Bureau, a total of $200 billion. The leading category of products sold by mail directly to the consumer is books and magazines. When we use the term "direct marketing," we include selling by direct-mail packages; catalogs of all kinds, some nine thousand at the last count; and coupon advertising in magazines and newspapers. U.S. direct marketers spend about $10 billion every year in the attempt to snare buyers for their products. This is a field of considerable importance to book publishers.

In mail-order publishing the most widely known players in the field are *book clubs.* These can be independently operated giants, like the two big leaders, the Book-of-the-Month Club and The Literary Guild of America, or spinoffs from national magazines, such as the *Reader's Digest* Condensed Book Club and the *Fortune* Book Club. They might also be part of a general publishing house like Bantam Doubleday Dell, which boasts seven core clubs, or retailers like Barnes & Noble. The field also includes such elaborate enterprises as Time-Life Books, an offshoot of Time-Warner, Inc.; and Grolier, Inc. Meredith's mail-order programs are operated by the corporation that publishes *Better Homes and Gardens.*

Some large general publishers have mail-order departments that not only sell the firm's books, but also originate titles of their own that lend themselves peculiarly to mail-order selling. They include information books designed to reach people with special interests who are not regular book buyers and who may never have been inside a bookstore.

There are also several kinds of subscription selling, notably the business of selling encyclopedias by mail and the merchandising of books (including dictionaries and encyclopedias) through supermarkets.

In terms of their share of the annual book sales volume, the books clubs and the mail-order publishers together have an almost equal portion of the market. The mail-order business continues to grow.

Book Clubs

The most familiar kind of mail-order selling is the book club. Among the many now in existence, the Book-of-the-Month Club (BOMC) is the colossus, and it was the first such modern enterprise. The idea, however, goes back to the early nineteenth century, between 1825 and 1850, when the American Tract Society, in the process of distributing millions of its products to a new mass market, invented a Tract-of-the-Month Club, and even gave bonuses for a certain number of purchases.

Book clubs of various kinds were tried with varying degrees of success until April 1926, when Harry Scherman devised the twentieth-century version that has been successful beyond even his most optimistic expectations. In its first six decades, it distributed more than 440 million books. The key to the success of the BOMC and several other clubs is what is called "negative option," a concept introduced by the great advertising genius Maxwell Sackheim of Schwab & Beatty. In brief, negative option is the practice by which a club member is sent the selection *automatically* unless the member sends in a card or order form *requesting that no book be sent.* The Fair Trade Commission registered a series of complaints about this system back in the 1960s; these were resolved to everyone's satisfaction.

There are approximately 150 book clubs listed in the current *Literary Market Place,* some with only a few thousand members, others counting membership in the millions. Some of these clubs are relatively new; others, like the Book of the Month Club and The Literary Guild, have been part of the American publishing scene for more than seven decades.

The Book of the Month Club (BOMC) and The Literary Guild, each with more than a million members, bring the newest and best fiction and nonfiction to their subscribers at a discount off the publisher's list price. Over the years, a number of clubs have evolved within the corporate structure of BOMC (a wholly owned subsidiary of Time-Warner) and also within the Guild (owned by the German publisher Bertelsmann). These offshoot clubs specialize in particular kinds of books—on crime or crafts, cooking or gardening, birds or computers. There are also clubs originating from professional book publishers that offer books in specific career areas. Professional book clubs, unlike the larger general clubs, direct their selections to specific fields of interest in the workplace. The largest professional group is the Newbridge Book Clubs, with sixteen professional clubs from the Architect and Designers Book Club to the Teacher Book Club. Book publisher McGraw-Hill and its Tab Books Division also run a number of professional clubs.

Especially worth singling out is the Quality Paperback Book Club, a part of corporate BOMC. QPB, as it's known in the trade, focuses on a largely youthful membership, with trade paperback editions of contemporary fiction and nonfiction, often before any paperback edition is available in the retail stores. There are also a number of children's book clubs for the home and classroom, as well as religion book clubs.

Altogether, the book clubs accounted for some $800 million in sales revenue of roughly 120 million titles and a market share of the billions spent by consumers for books of between 5 and 6 percent.

Book clubs are organized into four areas of operations: editorial, marketing, production, and fulfillment, with overall responsibility in the hands of supervisory management. The principal contact between the book publisher and the club is through the club's editorial staff interacting with the publisher's subsidiary rights department. Once the club editor and the publisher conclude their negotiations on a title, the club originates a contract spelling out the terms of the agreement: the advance, which may range from $1,500 to $2,000 for an unknown author to more than a million for a "star," bestselling author; the royalty scale; term of license; and selling territory. At the same time, the production department decides whether it will print its own club edition, using the publisher's film; "piggyback" on the publisher's print run; or buy copies out of the publisher's inventory.

The marketing departments include creative people who design and write copy for the bulletins, ads, new member mailing pieces, and so forth, plus those who work on finding new members through consumer advertising and mail-order solicitations. As competition between the clubs has increased, the marketing staff has come to play a much more important role in the business; the same situation is true among the book publishers, who more and more bring their editors into the marketing process from the beginning.

The fulfillment division of a book club, through its warehouse and shipping facilities, must process thousands of pieces of mail each day—orders, checks, queries, complaints—and dispatch thousands of books and bills. Except for the packing of books, all these operations are accomplished by computer, a development that has greatly enhanced efficiency.

Quite different from all other mail-order selling is the sort of mass-market merchandising done by Time-Life Books and Grolier Enterprises. These are publishing houses specifically designed to sell books by mail in a mass market, and their growth has been phenomenal since American Heritage began in 1954. (Grolier Inc. was founded in 1895, but its subsidiary, Grolier Enterprises, was created later.) Though these are the big leaders in the field, there are altogether some three hundred different firms listed in the *LMP* as subscription and mail-order book publishers, including those publishers, like Simon & Schuster and Van Nostrand Reinhold Co., who issue mail-order titles as well as general trade books.

Despite the high cost of putting selling materials in the mail and the high cost of producing the books and series themselves (Time-Life Books spends many hundreds of thousands of dollars testing and developing prospective programs, for example), the future appears bright. Telemarketing, or selling by phone, both by personal and computerized messages, is one development that has extended direct marketing companies' reach; computerized mailing lists have made the job of finding the right customers easier. Altogether the direct-mail industry now has a total of approximately fifteen thousand different mailing lists, available through some seven hundred list brokers. The largest list features *every name* in the country's five thousand telephone directories.

As a field for people who want to enter publishing, mail-order books offers many opportunities for jobs similar to those in other branches of the industry. Other jobs require a specific talent, like writing mail-order copy, and these positions are highly paid. Although trade publishing remains a training ground for this field, is is just as possible to get a beginning job and learn about the industry in mail-order publishing. Whether you should try it depends on whether you think this way of producing and selling books appeals to you more than others do. It is an extremely creative field.

BOOK PACKAGERS/PRODUCERS

Most book packagers deal with nonfiction projects, often as part of an established series of books. They usually contract with the writer on a flat fee basis, rather than royalty, and retain the copyright. Book packagers often seek out writers to do a nonfiction book. They attend writers' conferences, read the acknowledgments in books in fields that interest them, study special interest magazines and other periodicals, and call universities and colleges to find out who the experts are in various fields.

Book packagers need all the publishing personnel to deliver a finished product to the publisher with which they have contracted.

SUBSIDY AND COOPERATIVE PUBLISHING

While the vanity presses have little use for editors—they accept any manuscript a writer wants to pay to have published and provide minimal editing services—and no use for marketers—in subsidy publishing marketing, distribution, and sales all fall to the writer—cooperative publishers generally do employ a range of publishing personnel. Those involved with subsidy publishing earn their income from the writer. They produce a book to order, print the specified number of copies, and arrange for their delivery to the writer. Any income from sales the writer generates stays with the writer.

Cooperative publishers generally share the expense and the risk with the writer. They provide a full range of services, from editorial to printing, or sometimes work with camera-ready copy the writer has provided. Often they produce and distribute a catalog of their books.

As mentioned previously, often many small publishers work in three categories, publishing some books on a commercial basis, some with a co-op deal, and still others on full author subsidy.

ELECTRONIC PUBLISHING

There are two main types of electronic publishing:

1. Print on demand. Publishers, distributors, and booksellers now have the capability to print economically single copies of a book upon request by a consumer.

2. Online sale of books. Electronic versions of books may be ordered directly from publishers or from companies such as barnesandnoble.com, to be read on handheld electronic reading devices known as e-books. Though these devices are still expensive and certain technical problems remain, there is no question that the price will come down and the quality will go up, and portable e-books will eventually win consumer acceptance. But will they replace print books? That is doubtful. Book lovers still cherish the feel and smell of a book printed on paper. In the decades

to come, e-books might become more prevalent, but consumers will still demand printed books.

Some writers offer their work online, directly through their own websites, or through websites set up to cater to this new market. For a fee, writers can upload anything from poetry and journal entries to sample chapters or complete manuscripts of novels. The hope is to sell their material to customers, who simply download the file and read it from their computer screen or print it out, using their own paper.

Many new electronic publishing companies, such as industry leaders Hard-Shell Books and New Concepts, offer to post the writer's book for free and pay royalties. But is anyone buying books this way? It's hard to say. Electronic publishers can make money from uploading and editing fees, but no accurate figures are yet available on actual sales and profits.

Some sites offer to showcase the writer's material to prospective agents or traditional publishers, thus bypassing the tedious process of querying and proposing the traditional way, through regular mail. Writers pay a fee for this service, but editing is rarely provided.

Electronic publishing has brought attention to the problems of inadequate copyright laws covering this new field. While the copyright laws apply to material published online, just as to any other kind of publication, they are so far much harder, if not impossible, to enforce.

All things considered, electronic publishing is a force not to be ignored; it is most likely here to stay. Whether it will flourish and provide ample career opportunities remains to be seen.

CHAPTER 2

A CAREER IN BOOK PUBLISHING

THE CLIMATE OF BOOK PUBLISHING

"To those of us who practice publishing," the head of a major publishing company once wrote, "it is a curious, crazy, beloved, incomparable, frustrating, maddening, demanding, compelling—business or art or profession or job. Which is it? It is, at its best, a vocation." Surely, book publishing *is* a vocation—we could use the synonym "calling" to describe it—for many of the people who work in it. It can and should be much more than just another way of earning a living. Though not at every level the best paying field of work, nor by any means the worst, it does offer satisfactions and rewards that other occupations do not provide. And it attracts people who are willing to make it a lifetime commitment.

But *is* it a profession, like law or medicine, and what are the requirements for practicing it? Or is it strictly a business? Industry analyst John P. Dessauer describes book publishing as:

> ...both a cultural activity and a business. Books are vehicles of ideas, instruments of education, and vessels of literature. But the task of bringing them into existence, of purveying them to their readers is a commercial one requiring all the resources and skill of the manager and entrepreneur. It is appropriate, therefore, to describe book publishing as a *cultural industry.*

In that respect, it is much more like the theater, film, and record businesses than law or medicine, neither of which, of course, are free of commercial considerations.

For many reasons, most graduating seniors don't think of book publishing as a possible career choice. This is undoubtedly because publishing has a low public visibility. Book publishers have not been rendered glamorous in movies and television series, as have advertising executives, newspaper reporters, and magazine editors. Also, Americans are not predominantly book readers, and there is little public curiosity about the people who publish books. Individual authors become famous, but no one outside the business hears of their editors. Few people can identify the publisher of the book they have just finished reading. Students are likely to be bored with books by the time they graduate, and the idea of making more books fails to fascinate them. In addition to this lack of interest, there is a widespread ignorance of how books are created.

Because they have so little knowledge of what book publishing is about, students who may consider entering the field tend to think of it in terms of editorial jobs. Becoming an *editor* seems very exciting and may be the only publishing job they know about.

There is some confusion about writing and editing in publishing, as there is about the same two functions in magazine work. They are different occupations requiring different talents. Of course, some editors are good writers as well, and there are editor-authors on the staffs of both book publishing houses and magazines. They are, however, in a rather small minority. Serious writers of fiction would be better to get another kind of job than editing to support themselves while they struggle for recognition, as most of them must do. Nonfiction writers need much more time for research than publishing or magazine jobs usually afford.

That is not to say there is no room for writing talent in publishing. Editors need to be able to express themselves clearly and effectively in writing as they produce reports on the manuscripts they have been reading or outline book ideas for consideration. There are also specific writing jobs in the publicity and promotion departments, where press releases and similar materials are prepared. People who can write advertising copy will be able to use that talent in houses that produce their own advertising. But, basically, book publishing is not an occupation for people who want to be professional writers.

Nor is editorial work the only job possibility for those who want to get into publishing. Making books requires a variety of talents—the copyeditor who prepares the manuscript for the printer; the art department, which is responsible for cover and illustrations; publicity and promotion people; the production department, which designs and manufactures the book; and the sales department. There are many jobs within these various categories, and, in addition, a book publishing house must have the professional and clerical people required by every business: accountants, secretaries, bookkeepers, personnel specialists, receptionists, and mail room and shipping department employees. These jobs may seem remote from the excitement of the editorial department, and not many applicants are willing to start at them; however, publishing is full of editors and editorial executives who learned the business by starting, if not at the bottom, at least a long way from their ultimate professional goals.

PERSONAL QUALIFICATIONS

What should you ask yourself before deciding on a career in the publishing field? Is it enough, for example, just to "like books"? Not in the opinion of those who do most of the hiring. Few approaches turn them off more quickly than the applicant who says, when asked why he or she wants to get into publishing: "Well, I like to read." It goes without saying that anyone who *doesn't* like to read, who would rather watch television than read a book, is not a likely candidate for a publishing job. No matter what route you choose to reach the top in publishing, it is virtually impossible to succeed without being at home with the written word in all its shapes and forms, and without a high regard for the people who do the writing—and who are going to read it after it is written.

Along with that essential respect for the written word goes an interest—more like a *passion*—for detail. If this trait seems incompatible with the sensitivity and introspection implicit in being a "word person," no matter; that's the paradoxical nature of the publishing business. If we seem to stress the word *business* excessively in this book, do not be put off. Publishing is also an art and a science and a legitimate branch of culture that cuts across every human interest.

Here are some of the traits that any candidate for a publishing job should have:

Energy and stamina.   Publishing is not always a "9 to 5" kind of job. If that's what you're looking for, better look elsewhere. Book publishing people—editors in particular—are usually too busy in meetings, on the phone, or in planning sessions to do much reading in the office. That means taking manuscripts home. In order to meet deadlines, you may have to stay late or work on weekends. And you'll need to be able to work under pressure, which calls for energy and stamina as well as patience and unflappability.

Education.   A good liberal education is what most publishers are looking for in prospective employees. It doesn't hurt to have specialized in the physical or social sciences or in business or accounting, but generalists are more the rule than the exception in publishing.

Imagination.   Publishing has been called "a contest of ideas." The more ideas you have to offer, the more valuable you will be to a publisher and the more rapidly you will climb the ladder. Employers are looking for self-starters, people who bring in suggestions, not those who wait around to be told what to do. It also helps to know how to *present* your ideas—to be articulate, well organized, well spoken, and sincere in your convictions.

Business savvy.   Though you may run into the old "we can't hire you because you don't have any experience" line, don't be discouraged. That excuse is a dodge for personnel directors who don't want to say "there are no openings today," or "I really don't know how to place you in our firm." If you've had any kind of part-time or summer job at all—whether it was waiting on tables or clerking in a store—you've learned something about dealing with the public, and that's what business is all about: selling yourself and selling products. Lead from strength and with confidence that any business experience you've had will be useful. As an entry-level candidate you won't be expected to have years of practical experience—and you won't be competing with five- to ten-year veterans who do. Stress whatever your college major was, and don't be ashamed of your part-time jobs. You see—you *have* had experience!

Curiosity.   Try to be one, in Henry James's apt phrase, "on whom nothing is lost." All experience can be valuable to you in publishing, which deals with so many subject areas. All your reading, television viewing, and theater and movie going—they're grist for the mill. It's important to use your peripheral vision as well as seeing steadily and straight ahead. You never know when and where a good idea is going to come to you. Nor is there ever such as thing as "knowing too much." As for your hobbies or specialized interests, they too may become the building blocks of your publishing career. Ski buffs have found niches working for the many magazines devoted to that sport, or writing or publishing books on the subject. Will Schorz, crossword puzzle editor of the *New York Times,* parlayed his favorite pastime, solving and creating word games, into a successful career as a "cruciverbalist."

PERSONAL REQUIREMENTS

There are certain fundamental, practical assets that most people coming into publishing should have. To begin with, in today's technological world it is necessary to know how to operate a computer. It has become as essential a skill as typing has always been, and since the keyboards of a typewriter and computer are the same, it is easy to use the computer if you already know how to type. Courses and handbooks of all kinds are available for computer neophytes. Familiarity with the Macintosh or IBM Windows or both are highly recommended before you apply for that first job.

It is also helpful for those who aspire to editorial publishing careers to be able to write clearly and effectively. Editors write reports on the manuscripts they read, and there is a great deal of correspondence with authors. Writing promotion and advertising copy, of course, is a special skill for which good, clear writing is the basis. The late E. B. White, one of *The New Yorker*'s earliest and best writers and editors, was forever preaching the virtues of the simple, declarative sentence, which is the essence of that magazine's style—and is the kind of useful writing people coming into publishing need.

Another asset that those considering publishing careers seldom think about is good telephone manners. A great deal of business is conducted by phone, and it helps to develop an easy, persuasive telephone style, which can be done simply by working at it, without being self-conscious.

WOMEN IN PUBLISHING

Someone once described the ideal publisher as a "cultured statesman and a farseeing businessman." Let us amend that to read "businessperson." It is almost completely superfluous to say that publishing is a woman's as well as a man's world. On the contrary, there are few areas other than publishing in which women have made such vast and rapid strides. As William H. Scherman points out in his book *How to Get the Right Job in Publishing:*

> More than half of the 72,000 employees in book publishing are women. Women MBAs are taking on management and planning assignments; women publishers start their own magazines; women's by-lines originate more and more from the news capitals of the world rather than from only the kitchen and kindergarten.

CHAPTER 3

PREPARING FOR A CAREER IN BOOK PUBLISHING

If few graduating seniors think of publishing as a career, it is largely because it is the only profession that has no formal academic curriculum. Journalism, its closely related field, is taught at more than 150 accredited schools and departments of journalism in the United States. There are also graduate journalism programs leading to the master's and doctoral degrees in many universities. In short, it is a recognized academic discipline.

Book publishing, on the other hand, can boast of only a relatively small number of courses designed for the book trade, and not all of them are directly related to publishing careers. As the Association of American Publishers put it in its study of publishing, *To Be a Publisher:* "For decades attempts to educate people for publishing and to train those already in publishing have been, with few notable exceptions, sporadic, scattered, hit or miss. The occasional seminar, the infrequent book or essay, cooperation with a few institutions of learning."

Two common practices of staffing publishing positions still currently exist. Editorial personnel are recruited from a pool of college graduates who "care deeply about books." Management personnel, on the other hand, are:

> ...recruited from the graduate schools and from the experienced ranks of other kinds of business. Often members of the publishing community are isolated from one another. Editors may not understand the practicalities of production; sales representatives may not recognize the alliance between sales and promotion and subsidiary rights; editorial or publicity personnel may be unaware of how an order is taken or processed. Particularly disturbing is a too common ignorance of contracts and finance by people whose decisions are determined by contractual and financial considerations—decisions that may affect the profitability of a given project and even the economic health of the publishing house itself.

(To Be a Publisher)

This situation is changing, however, as publishing courses proliferate in the universities. A particularly heartening development took place in the fall of 1985 when Pace University in New York City began offering a master of science degree in publishing, the first program of its kind since the New York University Graduate School of Book Publishing was discontinued twenty-five years ago.

Publishing has traditionally acquired its recruits by doing nothing, permitting itself to be overwhelmed every June by job applicants, mostly from Eastern colleges and universities. From these, only a few were chosen. There were no prevailing standards, no prerequisites in general use; publishers were—and to some extent still are—as much individualists in this matter as they are in everything else. They are about where the journalism business was fifty years ago in its relationship to journalism schools. Those schools now supply a major part of the annual new recruits to newspapering; it is reasonable to believe that the same thing will be true for the book industry.

Signs of a change of heart in this regard are already evident. In recent years, personnel directors have found that the flood of applicants for jobs in early summer has lessened to a trickle, either because potential employees have been discouraged by reports of low salaries and difficulty in finding openings or because young people who might have been attracted to book publishing have preferred to go into some other business field. If enough book publishers discover that they cannot fill the three thousand to four thousand positions that open up in the book industry each year, they may begin to think it is more desirable, if not essential, to support educational programs in publishing whenever and wherever they can, and to encourage training programs of their own.

Formal academic training in the specific field is not essential, of course, to get a job in either publishing or journalism. Many people get into these fields with no more than the usual general liberal arts or some other college background, and there are even a few who get in without having gone to college at all. But preprofessional training, if it is done on a high level, can save you four or five years of career time and make you much more valuable to an employer.

COLLEGE MAJORS

What courses should a student take in college, if publishing is to be the career choice? The answer used to be, without question, enroll as an English major. This is still the answer if it is the field that interests the student most. But majors in other fields are just as welcome in publishing as English majors, and in fact, specialization in other fields can provide essential background for such areas as religion or textbook publishing, among others. People who plan to go into sales and distribution need to take marketing and related courses, while those interested in production will want to do all the graphic arts work they can.

A major in religion can lead to a job in religion publishing; one in economics can lead to a career in business books, textbooks, or publishing management. Any of the humanities is a good background for editorial work. A major in political science, for example, or history, with a minor in English, would be a good preparation. In fact, since publishing is so diversified, a college background in almost anything can be a preparation for a publishing career.

PROFESSIONAL TRAINING PROGRAMS

Specific professional training will give the job applicant something more than an academic degree to offer a potential employer. There are now a considerable number of choices for this training, where only a few existed a decade or so ago. Most of the best are in New York City, the center of the publishing industry.

New York University was an early pioneer in publishing education, having started its first extension course in the field in 1943. The NYU Center for Publishing, a part of the School of Continuing Education, offers evening courses throughout the year in copy editing and proofreading, book production and manufacturing, and book editing. In the late 1970s, NYU also offered an intensive one-year series of courses leading to a diploma in book publishing. This diploma program was designed for people already working in the field who wished to enhance their skills—but it was discontinued because of a lack of financial support. (Some, though not all, publishers have tuition payments for job-related courses as a regular part of their employee benefits.) A similar diploma program in magazine publishing is still offered.

The Gallatin Institute of New York University offers an M.A. degree program, as does Pace University. The stated goals of Pace's program, which leads to a master of science degree, are "to help fill the publishing industry's need for professionally trained personnel and to offer training in all aspects of book and magazine publishing." And since 1980 the Department of History at Arizona State University has offered a special graduate program in conjunction with a master's degree called "Scholarly Editing and Publishing Procedures."

A list of universities and other institutions offering courses in publishing is provided in Appendix B.

GETTING STARTED

In recent years, according to Chandler B. Grannis in his pamphlet *Getting into Book Publishing* (distributed by R.R. Bowker), a dozen people at different levels were asked how they got their first jobs in the industry. Some of the replies, reported at an annual meeting of the Association of American Publishers, were these:

"I volunteered."

"Help-wanted ad."

"By knocking on a lot of doors."

"By accident."

"I'm a member of the family."

"Eleven rejections and an acceptance."

"Through my college placement service."

"I was asked."

"Off the street."

"Through an endless series of tenuous connections."

And, finally: "I bought the company."

All of these answers include one piece of happenstance or serendipity—the person involved was there "at just the right moment." This may have been the result of luck or more probably planning, determination, and alertness.

Many publishers can report, "Someone I knew gave me a letter to someone he or she knew in the book business"—in other words, good old American "know-who," which never hurts. It is important at the beginning to use any and all personal contacts one has.

Other publishers can say, "I had some good recommendations and a good resume, and the company's personnel department was interested." Resumes are essential, and it is important that they be well organized, neat, and letter-perfect; nothing will cause a prospective employer in the publishing business to lose interest faster than a typo in your resume. (Two good sources on writing resumes are published by VGM Career Books: *Resumes for Communications Careers* and *Resumes for College Students and Recent Graduates.*)

At some point, you'll undoubtedly have to go through the personnel department, but it helps if you can make your first appointment with the person who will actually be doing the hiring. In most cases, that will be the head of a department. The jobs most commonly filled by personnel directors (or directors of human resources, as they are now most commonly called) are clerical in nature—typists, secretaries, and bookkeepers.

In general, it's good to have something useful to offer, based on a sound educational background. One ought to be able to present oneself straightforwardly, listen well, answer directly, and write clearly. Help wanted ads, and in major metropolitan areas, specialized placement agencies, may be consulted (although they are more useful for people already in the field looking for more advanced work).

"Training programs" vary from the publishing house where a new employee was told how to answer the phone and that his boss liked his coffee regular, to a paperback house where the initiation was an encouraging one, involving everything from a thumbnail lecture on ISBNs (International Standard Book Numbers) to a tour of the printing plant.

Applicants, particularly young women, but young men as well, are sometimes told that the way to get into publishing is to be a secretary. "Take word processing and shorthand," publishers say, "and they will get you your first job faster than anything else." That may be true, but these jobs do not always lead to advancement. Sometimes publishers take advantage of the eagerness of people to get into publishing by assuring them that the secretary's desk is a guaranteed avenue to success. They predict that the new employee will soon be in the editorial department, which usually is her or his ultimate ambition. Some publishers solve their always-difficult secretarial problems by promising these opportunities when they are hiring, with no intention of following through. This is particularly true if the secretary happens to be a good one—because competent secretaries are very hard to find.

Still, it must be admitted that there are few positions in which an employee can learn as much about the operation of a publishing house, or any other business, than as an executive secretary to the publisher. And more than one bright and ambitious secretary has parlayed that job into a much more lucrative and responsible position. It is possible to say that "the breaks often start where the buck stops"—in the chief executive's office.

People often are advised to start their book publishing careers in the sales department. They may have little taste for that kind of work, but this is nevertheless excellent advice. Sales rep jobs have a distinct advantage as a way into publishing: they pay better than do other entry-level positions.

There is no better way to learn about publishing than to sell books, and one could do worse than spend some time clerking in a bookstore—a truly educational experience for anyone planning to enter publishing and especially valuable for the editor-to-be. All the many aspects of book publishing come together at the point of sale, where the efforts of every department of the house are rewarded or not by the ultimate customer.

In the textbook field, the customary entry point is through sales, particularly in the college field, where travelers get the same valuable point-of-sale experience the bookstore clerk obtains. A majority of executives in the major textbook houses began their careers in the sales department.

The industry as a whole, though, needs all kinds of skills, not simply editorial ability and taste. There are jobs open in sales, administration, publicity and promotion, advertising, and production, but as one retired industry executive commented: "Those are jobs hard to fill at the basement level. We don't have good in-house training programs for them and so we tend to bring in only experienced people." In spite of this admitted obstacle, however, more recruits are coming into publishing than ever before through these noneditorial jobs.

Qualified and experienced professionals in a variety of fields are always welcome in publishing. *Accounting* is one such field. In any business there are the "sellers" and the "counters," those who make the profits and those who count them. Anyone with experience as an accountant in almost any field knows the jargon, the ins and outs of the trade, and should be able to fit easily and quickly into a book publishing house. *Artists* are needed in publishing in many different ways. Though many talented practitioners of the graphic arts prefer to work freelance, the larger publishers maintain full-time art staffs and are always looking to fill basic jobs as well as directorships. Other kinds of specialists are also always in demand, among them *librarians, computer technicians, website designers, researchers, lawyers, graphic arts or production experts, promotion writers, personnel executives, salespeople,* and, lest we forget, *merchandisers.* Today the products of book publishing houses—though not as mass market as toothpaste and cereal—are at least mass enough to attract executives from Proctor & Gamble and General Foods. So if you are an M.B.A. with some experience in the product managing area of some large manufacturer, there are areas in book promotion departments where you would be valuable—especially in the mass-market paperback field.

SALARIES AND UNIONS

Publishing is increasingly a young person's business, which is paradoxically a handicap to the young who want to enter it. Until the 1960s, it was predominantly a business of middle-aged and older white men, with women and minorities having hardly more than a foothold in it. The number of women and minorities in publishing has increased dramatically and the average age level of employees has dropped. Now those in their midforties predominate.

When the age factor is combined with the general contraction of the industry because of mergers and acquisitions, which tend to shrink the number of jobs available in the larger merged firms, it becomes clear that young people entering publishing will have to expect to spend more years at the lower levels than they did in the 1960s before they can get better jobs and more money. Jobs in book publishing, while improving somewhat, are still notoriously low-paying.

But that has always been the case in publishing. Even in 1776, when the first printer's strike in America closed New York's print shops briefly, the wages the printers were striking for and getting represented considerably more than the income of those workers in the publishing business who supplied them with the material to print. Many, if not most, authors wrote for nothing, and even at the end of the nineteenth century, it was still not at all uncommon for writers to subsidize their own books, even when they were issued by the best publishers.

This dismal history is no consolation to book publishing workers today, but they live with the salaries because they want to be in publishing, impractical as that seems to labor leaders.

According to the 1999 Association of American Publishers, Inc. (AAP) survey, compiled by Buck Consultants, entry-level assistants earned a median base salary of $25,500, as compared to $22,600 in 1997. Executive editors were at the top of the earning ladder. In 1999 their median salary was $90,000, a rise from $88,900 in 1997. Other categories of editors—senior/managing/acquisitions, etc.—earned $43,300 in 1999, a rise of $3,600 from 1997. And copy editors ranked between editorial assistants and senior editors, earning a median salary in 1999 of $34,300 ($31,200 in 1997).

The survey also provided 1999 median salary figures for sales reps:

Entry level: $35,400 ($29,200)
Journey level: $44,800 ($39,000)
Senior level: $51,900 ($49,000)

The figures in parentheses are the 1997 median salaries, showing that salaries are not stalled at any particular level.

At first glance, the salaries don't seem too dismal, until you factor in that most publishing positions are in New York, a city with an above average cost of living. But, offsetting the fairly low pay, respondents to an earlier study conducted by *Publisher's Weekly* report a high level of job satisfaction and a pleasant work atmosphere that allows for creativity.

CHAPTER 4

JOBS IN BOOK PUBLISHING

Jobs in book publishing overlap, as the preceding chapters make clear. No matter what kind of books a publisher may be producing—trade, religion, technical, texts—the individual jobs of the editor, the production people, the sales and promotions departments, the publicity people, and the others are basically the same from house to house.

From the employee's standpoint, this means that whatever is learned at one house can be applied in another. To examine publishing jobs in detail, then, a description of what happens in trade publishing will apply, with variations, to the other specialized divisions.

THE PUBLISHER

The *publisher,* or head of the house, may bear the title of *president, general manager,* or *chief executive officer.* Whatever the title, he or she has the responsibility for all company policies, including the planning and development of publishing objectives as well as administration of investment, staff direction, and budgetary and financial control.

The publisher in a large, publicly held corporate enterprise like Simon & Schuster (a subsidiary of VIACOM) will sit on the board of directors of the parent corporation and will report to the board and through the board to the stockholders. The publisher will be appointed by the board to run the company, with a contract for a specific number of years outlining compensation, benefits, stock options, and so forth. This CEO's perks may include a company car, country and city club, and perhaps an apartment for entertaining.

A publisher of a small house will probably be the owner or a partner of the company and may have come up through the ranks. There is no specific career path to the top, though usually the publisher will have had financial, marketing, or sales experience—less often, the publisher comes up through the editorial department. All the characteristics of a good editor as well as those of a good manager will stand the publisher in good stead, and her or his tenure and financial rewards will depend on imagination, innovation, continuity of programs, and, of course, ROI (return on investment) and profit performance.

This is the most coveted, rewarding, and demanding position in a publishing house. There is no reason for anyone starting at the bottom of the ladder *not* to aspire to become a publisher, even if the chances are slight of making it. Somebody has to do it—so why not you?

THE EDITOR

In any house, the publishing process begins with the manuscript—getting it and shaping it toward publication. That is the *editor*'s job. It could be argued that the editor holds the most important position in the house, since without the editor's work there would be nothing to design, sell, or promote. In specialized firms there is some uniformity in the editor's work—textbook editors, for example, work in pretty much the same way, whether in a large or small house. No such standard pattern emerges in trade publishing because practices vary from house to house. Nevertheless, the basics are the same, and what is described here can be taken as the average.

Executive editor or *editor-in-chief.*   Most houses have an executive editor, or more commonly, an editor-in-chief, and some have both. The *editor-in-chief* is usually the principle editorial figure, working closely with the publisher and with the other executives. If there is an *executive editor,* he or she is customarily one rung down the ladder and executes the orders of the editor-in-chief.

Managing editor.   Working directly below the editor-in-chief is the managing editor, who is a kind of traffic cop for the department. It is the managing editor's task to know where every manuscript is at any given moment after it has been accepted—whether it is being copyedited, being designed, in production, or being printed. The managing editor coordinates the editorial and production schedules, an extremely difficult job in itself, and in some houses he or she may work with authors or route incoming manuscript to editors.

The complexity of the managing editor's job in its most important aspect—coordinating schedules—illustrates the special abilities he or she needs.

Scheduling cannot begin properly until the manuscript is in house. Then it must be read, approved, copyedited, and sent into production. Four schedules are involved here: editorial, copyediting, design, and manufacturing. Three are flexible, but the fourth, involving printing and binding, is not, because binderies and printers work on crowded, tight schedules. Every delay adds to the cost of the book. It is easy to see, then, how important the managing editor's job is as he or she tries to keep the book moving through the whole editorial and manufacturing chain with the fewest possible delays. Few books present no problems along the way. There may be an editorial problem, with last-minute rewriting; or the copy-editor may need more time for a complicated book requiring research; or the author may spend too much time reading the galley proofs; or the printer may be having labor or equipment or delivery problems. Sometimes the list of hazards seems endless to the harassed managing editor. It is not an easy job, and it requires a general knowledge of the entire business and an ability to deal with a variety of people at several different levels.

Other editors.   Below the editor-in-chief and the managing editor in the publishing hierarchy come *senior* or *staff editors, associate editors,* and *assistant editors,* followed by *editorial assistants,* beginners whose duties are primarily administrative.

Literary agents or authors submit manuscripts or proposals to acquisitions editors to evaluate for publication. When a manuscript or proposal is considered acceptable for publication, the editor writes a proposal for it. He or she describes the book, tells something about the author, the market, the competition, and offers the other editors an opinion of the book and why it deserves publication. If the other acquisitions editors agree that the proposed book is a good fit for the publishing house's list, it is then moved forward for discussion at the editorial board meeting.

Editorial board meetings are usually held once a week. The publisher presides, and the books that are up for acceptance are considered. By this time, the various proposals have been read by all the others. Sales managers and publicity and promotion chiefs are included in these conferences. The question of whether to accept a manuscript is argued, but the process varies. In some houses, a majority vote to accept is required, although the publisher has the power to overrule the majority. In others, a single editor may take the responsibility for acceptance on her or his own shoulders, even though others are opposed to publication of the book. There are houses in which these editors are known as *sponsoring editors.*

The editor remains an integral part of the publishing process. In whatever framework the editors operate, they must eventually come to a decision about whatever manuscript is under consideration—whether to publish it. There is no magic formula involved in making these decisions, and nothing anyone who aspires to be an editor can learn beforehand will help, unless it is a wide acquaintance with books of all kinds. Only experience helps an editor estimate a book's possible sales, and even then one will frequently be wrong. Often the response is intuitive—a deep feeling that a book is good and worthy and needs to be published. Sometimes it is a calculated response—the conviction that book of a certain kind, or by a certain author, will have a profitable market. Occasionally (and more rarely, as time goes on) the decision to publish is made because the editor believes that a book deserves to be published for its literary merit, or in the public interest, whether it seems likely to make any money or not. Every editor of integrity, and every reputable publishing house, can point to selections made for this reason. The happiest circumstance for any editor, and it does come about, is when a book published on literary merit alone also becomes a bestseller.

THE COPY EDITOR

Copyediting is a kind of work virtually unknown to the reading public and often underestimated or misunderstood even by editors and others in publishing houses. In its basic form, it means taking the manuscript of a book and reading through it meticulously, correcting errors of spelling, usage, and grammar. At the same time, the copy editor is doing what is called *styling* the book for the printer. Publishers often have their own house style, and if they don't, copy editors use the standard guide, *The Chicago Manual of Style,* published by the University of Chicago Press. Styling means following accepted rules of punctuation, hyphenation, capitalization, indentation of quoted material, and similar matters.

If this were all there was to it, copyediting would not be the art that it is. Beyond the mechanics described above, there is the kind of creative copyediting that copy editors do for which authors and editors often ought to be more grateful than they are.

An author, for example, ought to be grateful for such routine creative copyediting as noting that a character's eyes are blue on one page and brown fifty pages later, that the steam heat is on when it is the middle of July, or that there are contradictions in different parts of the book in describing a character or an event. The author should be doubly grateful for the copy editor who takes a street guide to Paris, let's say, and follows a character's progress with it as the author describes movements in the city, to see whether the character could actually have passed the buildings or the streets or entered the restaurants where he or she is said to have gone.

Sometimes books require extensive research as copy editors check facts that raise questions in their minds. This is the part of the job that can't be learned. Superior copy editors have built-in alarm systems, bells that ring when they read a fact that seems possibly wrong. On an important book, where the greatest care must be taken, the copy editor's work may involve library research; therefore, among the qualifications for the job must be a knowledge of how to look up things and where to go to verify facts.

The copy editor is necessary because these errors *are* inevitable. Writers, however thorough their research or their perfectionist approach to their work, cannot avoid making errors in the course of hundreds of pages where they are setting down thousands of facts, whether real or fictional. The larger houses have their own copyediting staffs, but these companies have publishing lists so large that many manuscripts have to be "farmed out" to freelance copy editors. Smaller houses may have only one copy editor, or none, and must farm out everything. This has created a kind of job that may be done part-time at home, particularly valuable to people who have copyediting skills and who cannot, or who choose not to, work in an office. It provides part-time employment for a large number of people. Applicants usually are given the house-style book, if there is one, and a copyediting test to see if they have the skill needed for the work. If they do, they start with simple books. If they perform acceptably, they work up to the more complicated and important books.

THE DESIGNER

There were no professional *book designers* before the twentieth century because the printer, publisher, or both did the designing for themselves. In the early years of this century, most designing was done by commercial printers and binders, with the result that standards were low and the look of the books tended to be uniform and unimaginative.

The great change came in the 1920s, with the advent of such superior typographers and designers as W. A. Dwiggins, Daniel Updike, and other illustrious craftspeople. Today, nearly every house pays close attention to the design of its books, and many of them do outstanding work. Even textbooks, once the dreary products of utilitarian minds, are now often small works of art.

The purpose of design is to make the book attractive physically, to make it as easy to read as possible, and to make it meet the requirements of its particular market.

When the copy editor is finished, the designer takes over, to fit the manuscript into the number of pages the book is to occupy. The overall plan is determined by the book's budget, which has taken into account such factors as the estimated sale, the book's projected size, the number and character of its illustrations, the size of the first edition, the kind of printing process to be used, the kind of binding and paper, and the number of pages.

Designers plan the overall type design of the book, specifying the kind of type to be used for the text, for the chapter headings, the initial letters in chapters, the title page, even the titles that appear at the top of every page (known as running heads). Thus designers must, first of all, be typographers and also have some skill with mathematics, since the work often involves calculations. Though the book jacket is not always in the book designer's province, he or she must know how to make type alone, or type and photographs, achieve a maximum first impact on the prospective buyer. (Some jackets are designed by artists, usually outside the publishing house.) Since so much of this work involves printing and binding technology, the designer must be thoroughly grounded in those fields as well. Obviously, such knowledge is not acquired overnight. It is a truism in the business that good production people need at least two years of training.

The trend in publishing is toward having an art department in-house. Art departments get their recruits from the commercial art field, from printing and production establishments, and, of course, from other publishers.

Only the large houses have resident designers who do nothing else. Freelance designers are widely employed by others, but often design becomes a part of the art department's or the production department's work, depending on how the house is organized.

PRODUCTION AND MANUFACTURING JOBS

The production department of a publishing house is a collection of specialists. Smaller houses may not be able to afford production departments of their own, consequently either editorial employees are expected to perform these tasks or the work goes to professional production firms that service publishers.

The people in this community of specialists include *artists, designers,* and *typographers,* and sometimes specialists within these specialties. Production department heads work closely with the editorial department heads and the designer (whether in-house or freelance) in order to place the cost of production within the framework of the individual book's market and potential. This involves decisions about the kind of composition to be used, the printing and binding, types of materials to be employed, and the best use of available technology.

Production work is quite different from how it was years ago because technology has advanced so rapidly in recent years. Printing technology did not change appreciably between the fifteenth century and 1825, nor did modern printing methods begin to evolve until the early years of this century. But in recent years, the printing trade has galloped ahead at a breathtaking clip and is still changing rapidly. Many processes in common use today were hardly even contemplated in 1980, and more technical wonders are promised for the future.

Production workers need to have a variety of basic skills and a mastery of several areas of knowledge, as do designers. They must also have the ability to work closely with a small group of people, since production departments, on the average, consist of only four or five people.

The production people do the major part of their business with the book manufacturer, who sets the manuscript into type and then prints it in any one of several ways. While this is taking place, production sees to it that the illustrations are produced. All these steps in the mechanical production of the book must be synchronized so that the parts of the book—printed sheets, binding, and jacket—are brought together at the same time. That requires the application of a diversity of talents, and the production department must control these talents from beginning to end. Nothing can be left to chance; everything must be spelled out precisely. People who do not like detail, or those who are unable to handle it in a job, should avoid book production, because details are the lifeblood of this department.

In a sense, manufacturing a book is like putting a jigsaw puzzle together. Each step is related to another and all of them influence the cost of the book. Costs are important to everyone concerned with the book publishing process, and even a mistake of a fraction of a cent multiplies significantly over the course of a large printing.

SALES REPRESENTATIVES

The methods used to sell books vary with the subject and type of book being sold. The way textbooks, scientific and technical books, and religion books are brought to their point of sale is as specialized as these segments of the industry themselves.

We will talk here about how *trade* books are sold. A sales department can be large or small, depending on the size of the house, but it will always be headed by a *sales manager.* The smaller houses that are unable to afford a sales staff will have a sales manager who coordinates the efforts of commissioned sales reps on the road.

A sales department sells to *wholesalers, retailers* (bookstores), and *libraries,* for the most part, although it does fill individual orders. *Wholesalers* are the links between the publisher and the retailer, but these firms may also service schools and libraries. Like so many other aspects of publishing, there is no general agreement on who is and who is not a wholesaler, so it is difficult to talk about them in anything except general terms. There are specialists in this field—wholesalers who sell only paperback or medical books, others who sell only to schools and libraries, for example. A half-dozen or so handle the bulk of general trade books issued by publishers.

It is equally difficult to define a *retailer,* since there are bookstores that sell only books and others that sell a variety of goods; some are departments in retail dry goods stores, and others are college stores.

A sales representative who comes to work for a trade publishing house will be assigned a territory. At the beginning, it will probably not be in one of the most profitable parts of the country; veteran sales reps usually work in the more active areas. The sales rep on the road carries samples in a big bag—a few of the books themselves, jackets of others, descriptions of the remainder. The modern sales representative travels by plane, train, bus, and automobile from city to city, wherever there are bookstores.

Retail booksellers are usually very busy people, and the manager, owner, or whoever does the buying cannot give all visiting sales reps much time. The large or specialty houses get the most attention. In whatever time they have, sales reps have to display their wares and convince wary and skeptical book dealers to buy as much as they can without overbuying. Potential bestsellers, the work of noted authors with big sales records, and titles that fill a special need or interest are easy to sell. It is when it comes to other books on the list, by unknowns or on subjects that may not currently be in vogue, that the sales rep may have a hard time selling even one copy of a title.

The sales rep's lot is not easy, but it has its rewards. The sales rep becomes friendly with the booksellers—a rare, fascinating, and interesting breed—and these friendships on the road help to pass some lonely after-work hours. But the life has its frustrations, too, and only those attuned to the romance of bookselling in general remain to become veteran salespeople. Surprisingly, there are many of them—people who find this kind of selling more human, more varied (as books themselves are varied) than selling standardized products in the regular business world. Others use selling as a stepping-stone to editorial or other inside work, either voluntarily or because the house they are interested in believes that future editors or other employees ought to know what happens when books are actually sold to readers—a subject about which an astonishing number of people in publishing remain ignorant.

The sales department gets products from the editorial department and is required to sell them so that the business side of the house will be satisfied. The sales manager is an extremely important figure and consequently has a good deal of latitude in the firm. He or she is listened to at the editorial conferences.

Twice a year, sometimes more often, comes the ritual known as the sales conference. Before they go out on the road to sell the spring books, and later before the fall season, a conference for the sales reps is held, lasting from a few days to two weeks. The books they are going out to sell are presented to them by the editors at these meetings. Sometimes individual editors present the books of their authors; in other houses, the list is discussed in detail by one or more senior editorial executives, or perhaps by the editor-in-chief. Often an author is brought in to talk about a book, particularly if he or she happens to be a celebrity or a new and well-known author the firm has just acquired. This is also done if the book itself represents something unusual.

The purpose of this is to inspire the sales reps to go out and sell these books for which everyone on the editorial side is displaying such enthusiasm. In reality, it is an opportunity for the sales reps to have the list laid out before them and to make their own judgments about what they can sell when they are actually in the stores. Unfortunately for the authors, these judgments are made much more on the basis of sales potential than merit, although some books have both.

Sales reps who work on the staff of a house—there may be fifty or more in the largest houses—get a salary plus traveling expenses. Commissioned travelers, selling the lines of several houses, get a commission of 5 to 10 percent instead of a salary and pay their own expenses. There are selling organizations that offer such services on an organized basis, covering large geographical areas for publishers who can't afford their own sales staffs. The largest of these organizations have gross annual sales in the millions of dollars.

The chief requirement for a sales rep, aside from the ability to sell books, is a strong constitution. The bags are heavy, and the traveling is constant; the motels, hotels, and restaurants are not always first-class. In these days of jet aircraft, air-conditioning, and standardized chain hotel–motel service, the sales rep's life is easier than it used to be, but it is still a far cry from desk work in an office. Many sales reps prefer the job for precisely that reason.

SCHOOL AND LIBRARY SALES

Though many publishers have sales reps calling on schools and libraries, only the largest have separate sales forces for this work. The kind of books a house publishes is also a determining factor here. One that issues many reference books, for example, or books that can be used in school curricula will exert more effort in this market. Sales representatives in the field are called upon to do more than simply sell books. They have a service function, too, as they explain the firm's discount and order plans and help libraries get information about the new books that are particularly suited to the individual system.

This has led to a new specialty within the sales fields—*school and library consultant.* Many houses have such positions, and their importance has been growing for a decade or more. Such consultants spend a good deal of time visiting schools and libraries to get the kind of information about their needs that will enable their houses to serve them better. They are a kind of roving ambassadors, establishing lines of communication and spreading goodwill, if they can. They learn who buys the books for the school or library and how much money the buyer has to spend annually. Then they make sure these people get examination copies of books they might buy (and when they buy for a large library or school, the order may be for a hundred copies or more of a single title). In the office, they direct the flow of direct mail solicitation that goes continuously to schools and libraries, including catalogs and newsletters. If the house is small enough, they may do the writing of these mailing pieces as well. Finally, they help the house formulate advertising to reach this market through specialized magazines.

PROMOTION

Another function of the sales department is *promotion.* People who work in this area help sell books by methods other than advertising and publicity. They devise and produce things that will help the retail dealer sell the firm's books, including point-of-purchase display material, direct mail for dealers, booksellers' catalogs, exhibits of various kinds, and other merchandising devices, like contests. A few houses have separate sales promotion departments, but more often this is part of the sales or advertising department.

The amount of materials the people in the department are called upon to produce is extremely large, and the list of separate items seems endless: window stickers or streamers, posters, display racks, printed material that booksellers can mail to their customers, catalogs they can use in a similar way, and promotion ideas to sell a particular book.

A promotion department will probably be in charge of the firm's exhibits, although this may also involve the advertising, sales, and publicity departments in varying degrees. These exhibits are displays of the company's books at conventions of professional and scholarly organizations. Most of these conventions have what amount to book fairs, with the publishers displaying their wares in booths. Textbook houses dominate this kind of exhibition, but those with serious trade books to sell are represented, too.

Other conventions include the annual affairs held by booksellers, teachers, and librarians. The American Booksellers Association (ABA), the American Library Association (ALA), the National Association of College Stores, and the giant Frankfurt Book Fair all have huge exhibit areas where the books of most publishers in the United States and some foreign houses are displayed. The ABA and ALA conventions are attended by as many as thirty thousand industry people and provide a social meeting place for publishers and booksellers as well as a place to discuss the industry's problems.

ADVERTISING

Book advertising has several different functions. It exists primarily, of course, to sell books, and secondarily to help create a market for books. It is also designed to demonstrate to jobbers and retailers that a house is backing the titles it is selling and similarly, to convince authors and agents, who are not easily convinced, of the same thing. Advertising in trade journals helps reviewers to assess forthcoming books in a preliminary way, although it doesn't often influence them. Finally, book advertising helps in the sale of book club, reprint, and other subsidiary rights by keeping the book in the public eye while deals are being negotiated.

The advertising department in a trade house, like the other divisions, varies in its number of employees according to the size of the house. It may have as few people as one manager and a secretary or, more typically, an additional assistant and a typist or two. In a medium-sized operation, the secretary might be expected to keep cost records, tabulate returns from direct-mail campaigns, and perform similar housekeeping chores, while the assistant would be called upon to write catalog and jacket blurbs, copy for circulars and sales letters, and perform similar tasks.

In larger departments, people to do publicity and sales promotion might be added, and in technical, scientific, and educational houses, where special markets have to be reached, the department would have to expand to include more specialists. This would be the case in houses that do a great deal of direct-mail advertising. The largest departments have their own art staffs to lay out the promotional material and to design books and jackets.

A publisher may have a department as described above or may turn all advertising over to an agency that works through a liaison person in the house who may be called an *advertising manager.* Alternatively, a house may have a small advertising department of its own, consisting of one or two people, and turn part of the work over to an agency.

An advertising department manager has responsibilities that vary with the size and division of work in the department. In any case, the manager must supervise the operation, recommend how much money should be spent on individual titles, and often write jacket blurbs—the descriptive material about the book and its author that appears on the folded-in side panels and the back of the jacket. Sometimes this work overlaps that of the promotion department in producing special mailings and point-of-purchase displays. The ad manager has a responsibility, too, of seeing that the advertising reflects the view of a book held by the publisher, the editor, and the sales department.

Advertising managers have to be budget watchers, and the budgets are small. Few products made in the United States are placed on the market with so little advertising as are books. Publishers do not agree on whether advertising sells books or whether it does any more than bring a book to the public's attention. An advertising budget for a first novel, let us say, may be only $5,000 to $10,000—scarcely enough to do more than buy an announcement advertisement in a trade journal like *Publishers Weekly* or *Library Journal,* and perhaps one advertisement in *The New York Times Book Review.* Publishers do a great deal of what is called "list advertising," in which one advertisement displays several books, or often simply lists them, each with a brief descriptive paragraph. From the publisher's standpoint, the virtue of list advertising is that it at least mentions books that otherwise might get no display advertising at all.

With such budgetary limitations, the advertising manager has to plan very carefully, to get the most for the money, and often fend off indignant authors who want to know why their books aren't being advertised. These inquiries are passed on to the editor. Most authors are convinced their books would sell if the publisher advertised them, and the complaint is universal that they don't. It would be difficult, however, to prove that books, with some exceptions, can be sold by advertising. What advertising does is bring the books to the attention of prospective readers in the most attractive way possible, but no amount of advertising will sell a book people do not want to buy.

PUBLICITY

Publicity departments are founded on the premise that books are news, since they are carriers of ideas and information. The outlets for this news are the minority of newspapers (not much over three hundred) that carry book reviews, and the more numerous television and radio talk shows, which offer a virtually insatiable market for authors to talk about their books. These appearances are arranged by the publishers' publicity department.

Publicity work requires close cooperation with nearly every department in the house—editorial, sales, advertising, and promotion. The cooperation is closest, naturally, with the advertising and promotion departments, whose work it supplements.

One of the primary jobs of the publicity department is to send out review copies. This is not a haphazard business, by any means. The publicity director has *A* and *B* lists of reviewers, divided according to the size and influence of the media represented. The *A* list gets the books that are most likely to be reviewed and that the company is pushing most; the *B* list may get some of these, but mostly it is sent what remains.

Accompanying each review copy is a news release about the book (written in the publicity department), a photograph of the author, and sometimes a picture of the jacket. All this material is the responsibility of the publicity department. Review copies also go to the several publications that reach the book trade and provide short "forecast" reviews of leading titles. Publicity people have to be sure review copies reach their recipients in time to meet the reviewer's deadline and the book's publication date. Some book reviewers work weeks or months in advance of publication, and all of them want their copies at least a month before the book is released.

Besides the regular *A* and *B* lists, publicity departments have specialized lists of reviewers, like garden editors and editors of life-style pages, to whom books of special interest can be sent. A review of a special interest book, in fact, can be obtained in a publication that would not review any other kind of book except one dealing with its specialty. Newspapers that do not ordinarily review books, and that includes most of them, will review one by a local author, so the publicity department uses the questionnaire completed by authors about their backgrounds to get some attention in the places where they have lived.

Publicity people not only provide the usual releases with the books, but they send out special stories, pictures—anything that will call attention to the book. The eternal hope is that the department's stories will produce the most prized publicity—stories involving a book and its author that appear in the news columns. This is easiest to do, of course, when the book itself has news value, as in the case of one containing political revelations, or authors who themselves are news for one reason or another. Stories can also be suggested to magazines about authors who have attained some kind of literary achievement, like a Nobel or a Pulitzer prize, and for whom an overall view of their accomplishments would be apropos at the time of publication of a new book.

Another function of the department is to submit books for such awards as Pulitzer prizes and others. These prizes mean prestige for the publisher and the author and constitute a kind of public relations campaign in themselves, directed to other authors and agents. There are many of these honors available beyond the best-known ones.

Radio and television talk shows also provide numerous outlets for publicizing books. Whether they actually sell books is a matter of controversy, but the common belief is that anything that calls attention to a book cannot be bad. Publicity people who make these arrangements come to know a large number of people—executives, producers, commentators, television personalities, and their staffs—and become adjuncts of the broadcasting business. They often escort authors to the studios and stay with them during the broadcasts. Their days are filled with telephone conversations with the studios, "selling" authors to the programs, and making detailed arrangements for their appearances. At times, publicity people will "prep" authors for television appearances, grooming them, coaching them, and even preparing scenarios of prepared questions and replies that enable authors to get in frequent "plugs" for the book. To some of those who do it, it is a glamor job. Certainly it brings the book publicity person into close contact with the broadcasting business, and there is a certain amount of crossover into that better-paid industry.

Publicity people also arrange press conferences for authors, when a book is newsworthy, and they plan road trips when writers embark on promotional tours for their books. During these trips, the authors appear in bookstores for autographing parties and on local radio and television stations. The publicity department also works with clubs and organizations that sponsor book-and-author luncheons, making arrangements for authors to appear.

Finally the publicity department has a public relations function. Its people write releases telling about the activities of the house, and these are sent to publications reaching the trade and others serving the communications media. Another aspect of public relations is to keep a complete biographical file on authors, including reviews of their books, so that critics, scholars, reprint houses, and foreign publishers can have access to this information. As part of their general function, publicity people help promote such industry events as Children's National Book Week and National Library Week.

Sometimes a publicity manager will offload a campaign on one of the numerous independent publicists, most of them former in-house publicity managers or directors, who do all the same things the house might do, but work outside the house, for a fee. They are used when the house's publicity department is too busy to handle a major author; when the author is "difficult," necessitating an unwarranted amount of attention; or when the publicity must be done long distance, in Los Angeles, perhaps, or Chicago. The independents serve to supplement the publishing house's own efforts; occasionally they are hired by the authors themselves, who want extra attention. Whatever the arrangement, they work closely with the in-house publicity manager. These publicity firms are also always in the market for entry-level and experienced employees.

MANAGEMENT

In general, book publishing management jobs are what they would be in any business organization, but subject to the peculiarities of publishing, which set it apart from the others as an enterprise. A publishing house has *accountants* and people who take care of the *billing* and *shipping*. Shipping (called *fulfillment*) often is done by New York publishers from some point outside the city, because it is cheaper, more efficient, and more convenient than doing it in-house. Some publishers operate combined warehouses, but large orders usually go from bindery to customer without warehousing. The publisher or owner works closely with the business side of the company and is its chief executive officer.

Though a good many cases could be offered of people in the business department who used their jobs as entry points to editorial, advertising, or sales positions, they would be in the minority. By and large, those who enter publishing on the business side make their careers there, and when they rise in the firm, it is usually to executive management positions.

SUBSIDIARY RIGHTS AND PERMISSIONS

Most of those who contemplate entering publishing would never think of jobs in the *subsidiary rights* department, because few people outside the industry have any idea what these positions entail.

They are, however, highly important to the publisher financially. A substantial portion of a house's income is derived from the sale of those rights granted to the publisher by authors and their agents. Individual contracts specify how much the publisher's share of these rights will be, if any. They include first serial rights, meaning the publication of all or part of a book in a magazine or newspaper before the publisher issues it; book club rights; translation and foreign publications; second serial rights, meaning use in a publication *after* the book is published (usually bought only by newspapers); reprint rights; radio and television rights; motion picture rights; and dramatic rights. Of all these, the reprint right is today the most important because of the huge sums paid for them by paperback houses and because most book contracts give publishers a 50 percent— or more—share of the proceeds. They are often excluded from sharing in other rights, especially motion pictures, where sales figures can be high.

A much less exciting but necessary part of the department's work is the granting of permission to reprint. Sometimes the request is for extracts that other authors want to use as quotations. In other cases, the permission is asked by anthologists, and more important, by digest magazines and publishers of abridged books, like the *Reader's Digest* Condensed Book Club. Publishers must set fees for permission to reprint, although sometimes this is determined outside the house by holders of the copyright or the estates of dead authors. Rights and permissions department personnel have to consider each request made to it for a permission to use material. They must decide first whether to grant it, then set the fee and collect it. This involves a great deal of correspondence, and it is the largest part of the department's work. The job is a responsible one and offers a valuable specialization for people interested in this kind of work, which involves authors, agents, other publishers, magazines, and, in general, a variety of contact with many different people.

Large houses require several people in the department to handle the work, but the smaller ones usually make do with a single individual and a secretary. This is another part of publishing where there is really no substitute for on-the-job training. It is a complicated, detailed kind of work, and those who have no love for detail will be unhappy in it. Some legal training would help, but it is not essential by any means.

LITERARY AGENCIES

The importance of literary agents to publishers has already been noted; since they provide at least three quarters of all the general trade books published in America, they exercise an influence out of all proportion to their numbers.

There are some 240 agents who are members of the Association of Author Representatives (AAR) and scores of others who haven't yet qualified to become a member or choose not to join. (AAR member agents agree to adhere to the AAR Canon of Ethics.) You can learn more about AAR membership from visiting their website at www.publishersweekly.com/aar/. Their address is provided in Appendix A.

Most agents are based in New York City, although there are agents in virtually every large metropolitan area, especially Los Angeles.

Most if not all agents have probably worked for some time as editors in publishing houses, where they have established contacts with authors, contacts that stand them in good stead when they open their own offices or go to work for existing agencies. Some agencies, such as William Morris, are quite large, handling hundreds of authors of books and magazine articles; others are one- or two-person operations with little more than secretarial help and a battery of telephones. It is on the telephone that most agents do the better part of their business, or in meetings with publishers, which may take place anywhere from the editor's office to a lavish restaurant in midtown Manhattan.

Agents are invaluable links between the author and the publisher, providing guidance and advice to their clients, ensuring the best possible contracts they can negotiate for the books they handle, and, for the authors, serving as literary midwives, psychotherapists, nurses, and often close friends. For the publishers, they screen books that might otherwise wind up in the slush pile, and sometimes deliver books to a publishing house that have been preedited, saving the editor considerable time and effort. They also absorb the publisher's complaints or problems with an author, helping smooth over rough situations and avoiding author-publisher conflicts, which can be quite destructive. In every respect, they earn the 15 percent in commissions they get from an author's royalties.

There are many worse places to start in publishing than an agent's office. Not only will a neophyte learn a good deal about how publishers operate, but the people you meet can be very helpful in your publishing career—and there is as much movement from an agent's office to a publishing house as there is in the other direction.

PART TWO

NEWSPAPER PUBLISHING

CHAPTER 5

NEWSPAPERING AS A WAY OF LIFE

Newspaper work boasts one of the oldest, most well-known career traditions in American life. Since before the days of the American Revolution, the people who have devoted their lives to the work of a free press have found that the work has demanded a deep involvement.

To call working for newspapers a way of life instead of simply a career goes to the heart of what newspaper publishing is all about. It implies not only a commitment, the kind that would be required for going into the other professions, but a willingness to become a particular kind of person, one who becomes a trained observer of human events rather than a direct participant in them.

Newspapering is not all reporting what happens, by any means, as we'll see later on. Behind every man and woman who is out of the newsroom on assignment is a larger group of people—those who edit what is written, who decide what stories are to be covered, who process news that comes into the office from other cities and countries by wire, who take the pictures that go into the paper and edit them, not to mention the specialists who handle sports, theater, film, books, editorials, columns, and the other departments of a paper.

If you're planning on entering the newspaper business, you are about to join one of the largest industries in the United States. Like every other American business, it has grown from small beginnings and has changed radically with the times.

NEWSPAPERS IN NORTH AMERICA

Newspapers in the United States began as primarily propaganda organs, became the tools of political parties, evolved into the personal expressions of individual entrepreneurs, and eventually, in our time, became business institutions whose business was selling news and entertainment. The dividing line between magazines and newspapers has steadily narrowed until today they have become competitors in several ways.

The newspaper of today is still basically what it has been since 1835, that is, a vehicle to transmit local, national, and international news. But in the effort to compete with other media, notably magazines and television, it has been compelled to entertain as well as report news. In some newspapers today, entertainment outweighs the news content.

During the 1970s, the newspapers of this country and in other parts of the world began to undergo a technological revolution that is automating the production process and enabling editorial workers to employ electronic and other devices that make the newsrooms of even twenty years ago seem old-fashioned.

In the midst of all these changes, however, working on newspapers has not altered in its essentials from what it was a hundred years ago. Getting the news and printing it remains unchanged. It is only the means of transmission, from keyboard to delivery of the finished product, that are changing.

CHARACTERISTICS OF PEOPLE IN NEWSPAPER WORK

What do all these people have in common? First of all, they have a consuming curiosity about the world and everything that's in it. People who are not intensely interested in what goes on around them would be well-advised to go into some other field. Another primary characteristic of newspeople is something that used to be called "a nose for news," although this phrase isn't heard much any more. Whatever it's called, it is essential. You must know news when you see it. It's a difficult thing to define, although many people have nevertheless tried to define it. Obviously, a three-alarm fire, a murder, a natural catastrophe like a flood or a tornado, or a political leader accused of a civil or criminal offense—all these unquestionably constitute news. But one of the common definitions, "News is anything that happens," isn't quite accurate, because sometimes news is something that *doesn't* happen.

Another definition, "news is anything of interest," comes closer to the mark, if we define "interest" as involving the interests of large numbers of people. Thus, if Mr. and Mrs. Smith have a family quarrel, and Mr. Smith packs his bag and walks out, that is of no interest to anyone except the Smiths and their families, and possibly the neighbors. But if the quarreling couple happen to be celebrities, in show business or political life, a great many people are sure to be interested in the outcome, and so it becomes news.

What happens to people in public life is news, and so is anything that affects the broad interests of people—happenings in business and finance, sports, the arts, religion, politics, sex, and so on. The relative importance of these happenings to each other depends on the news judgments of editors, and among experienced professionals, these judgments are strikingly alike. A survey of the front pages of fifty newspapers on the same day has shown that the decisions about the relative importance of news items made by these editors were substantially alike.

Even the major exception was a consensus; some editors believe that any local story outranks a national or international event unless it is a major one.

Communication Skills

A necessary personal characteristic for people who want to go into the editorial side of newspaper work is the ability to effectively use the English language. This may seem obvious, but a common complaint of editors today about the young recruits they take on is their inability to spell and their ignorance of grammar. Not everyone who goes into the newspaper business has the same writing ability as far as style is concerned, but a reasonable minimum qualification for everybody would be an ability to use the language correctly.

No one should believe that the new "electronic newsroom" will relieve anyone of the need for basic skills. Newsrooms across the country have rapidly converted to video display terminals, but reporters using them to write their stories are still confronted with keyboards. We now have the ability to edit with an electronic pencil as well, but the skills that guide the pencil, the knowledge of spelling and grammar, are the same as they've always been.

Well-Rounded Education

People who like to work with words are invariably readers. Those who work on the editorial side of newspapers are usually well-read, and their tastes in reading are broad. They have a good background in history, especially American political, social, and cultural history, and know something about the other broad areas of human affairs. In fact, for newspaper writers, or writers in any other field for that matter, it is impossible to know too much.

Patience

Like the army, newspapering also requires people who are characteristically patient. There is a great deal of "hurry up and wait" in newspaper work. For every intensely interesting and important assignment, there are dozens of others that are boringly routine, and countless hours are spent in newsrooms waiting for something to happen on dull nights and Sundays.

Social Skills

Among the shared characteristics of newspaper people is a kind of generalized ability to get along with others, or at least to be the kind of person other people will talk to readily. Part of this is an art that can be learned from experience, but it is also a matter of personality. People who are shy and withdrawn, who find it hard to speak with others and especially to talk about anything that goes beyond everyday commonplaces, are not usually good reporters. A reporter should seem open and sympathetic. For example, one local reporter could cry at will, and if, for example, he was required to get information from a woman who had just lost her husband, he could sit down and seem to share her grief, meanwhile jotting down between sobs whatever she was able to tell him.

Physical Endurance

On smaller papers, another requirement is physical endurance. Most large dailies have contracts with the American Newspaper Guild specifying among other things, the hours reporters and other staff members can work—usually the standard eight-hour day, five-day week; no such limits exist on the nonunion papers. They work until the paper gets out, whenever that is, and stay with an assignment until the story is covered. Even on a weekly paper, there is enough to do to keep people busy six days a week and often parts of the seventh.

Dedication

Not everyone who goes into the newspaper business stays in it, but on the editorial side, there is probably less attrition than in most other occupations. That is because another characteristic of the newsperson is dedication to the job. In old movies about the newspaper business, there was often a sentimental old editor, or an idealistic young reporter, who talked about his devotion to "the newspaper game" with tears in his eyes. There was a grain of truth in this kind of melodrama. Nobody now calls it "the newspaper game," if they ever did; and tears were probably never shed for it. But there are thousands of editors and reporters working today who could conceive of no other way of making a living.

If students contemplating newspaper life understand that and know that the perennial fascination of newspaper life lies in always being close to what's happening whatever that may be, see themselves as the observer of events, and find any other way of life inconceivable, they are prime candidates for the field. For some, other ways of living *do* become conceivable, and people do leave newspapers for magazines, broadcasting, book publishing, or public relations, but they almost always carry with them some of that feeling for newspaper life.

Ask yourself if you fit this pattern and find out how you really feel about newspapering. Then consider the other qualifications we've discussed. If you've already said a resounding and emphatic "yes" to that first question, the others don't matter as much. You're committed—you're on the way to becoming a newsperson.

CHAPTER 6

THE SCOPE OF NEWSPAPER WORK

Newspapers are the least diversified of any communications medium, although the companies or corporations that publish papers may also own magazines, radio and television stations, book publishing houses, or any number of other businesses wholly unrelated to the media. For career purposes it is more convenient to talk here about newspapers alone, remembering that those who go to work for a large communications complex, beginning on a newspaper, may wind up in some other part of the conglomerate.

STRINGERS

To begin at the lowest rung of the ladder, stringers—those often unsung correspondents who work by themselves on space rates—have offered what may be the most common approach to getting into the newspaper business, at least for generations of writers. There is, of course, a hierarchy in the stringer system. At the bottom are young men and women still in high school who write school news for the local paper, sometimes without pay if the local editor is not above exploiting them. They may, at the same time, write local news items after school hours, thus working themselves into summer jobs on the paper.

If they happen to be doing this in small towns that have a county-seat paper nearby, they can begin sending in town news, for which they will be paid so much per column-inch for everything the editor uses.

WEEKLY NEWSPAPERS

Stringing is indeed the bottom rung of newspaper work, but it's a place to learn and a means of getting started. The next step is often a job in the next layer of the newspaper organization, the weekly paper. Weekly papers in small towns have proliferated since the advent of the photo-offset press, which makes it possible to start a newspaper for a fraction of what it once cost. Biweeklies, triweeklies, and even semimonthlies are included in the category of weekly papers, and there are more than eight thousand of them in the United States. Some are tabloids, others come in odd sizes like those on the islands of Nantucket and Martha's Vineyard, which are wider than the others; most, however, are the same standard size as their big-city counterparts. Many are small and struggling, getting by on eight or sixteen pages a week. Others regularly run thirty-six pages or more, and some large suburban weeklies have a hundred or more pages.

As the United States has become a country in which about 75 percent of the people live in cities or in the suburbs that ring them, the big metropolitan dailies have been in a slow decline, while the surrounding weeklies have gained in number and affluence. These suburban papers are primarily advertising media, but they also serve as community bulletin boards. In the small towns outside metropolitan circulation zones, the weeklies not only serve as bulletin boards but also record the life of the town in a way that big newspapers cannot do, even with the best of local coverage.

DAILY NEWSPAPERS

One step above the weekly is a less diversified and more homogeneous group, the daily newspaper, of which there are about seventeen hundred in the United States. These papers range all the way from the prestigious *New York Times* to dailies in towns as small as five thousand inhabitants or fewer. But whatever the size of the community they serve, dailies not only have their regularity of publication in common, but they have, generally speaking, the same format. The mavericks in the group stand out. The two major differences are whether they are morning or afternoon newspapers and whether they are tabloid or standard, meaning the full-size paper with which we are all familiar. All dailies operate around the clock with at least some kind of staff, but the morning papers concentrate their work from late afternoon to early morning and appear on the street and on their readers' doorsteps either sometime during the late evening or very early the next morning. Afternoon papers concentrate their efforts from early morning until sometime in midafternoon. Their editions usually begin appearing about 10:30 A.M., with finals in early or midafternoon—in any case, not too late to catch the outward flow of commuters.

The United States is a nation of morning paper readers. Nearly all of the best daily journals are in that category. Traditionally, afternoon papers are more lively in their news coverage, seeking to entertain more than instruct the home-going commuter or the person who picks up the paper after dinner. A large part of the information in afternoon papers is in the financial section, particularly closing prices on the stock exchanges.

Wire Services

An important part of the American press are the wire services. They supplement the news-gathering of the papers themselves, often supplying news from places geographically beyond a staff's coverage, at other times supplementing that coverage. The *New York Times*, for example, with the largest foreign and domestic news-gathering staff in the world, nevertheless uses not only the two major American wire services, but also the British, French, and several others. Not even the *Times* reporters can cover everything.

For daily papers that are not financially able to afford their own foreign staffs, or even correspondents in other American cities, the wire services are indispensable. Some major newspapers like the *New York Times*, the *Washington Post*, and the *Los Angeles Times* have their own wire services, selling the work of their columnists and reporters to other papers, some as far away as the *International Herald Tribune* in Paris.

Syndication

Syndication is another facet of the daily newspaper business. Large syndicates like United Features and King Features sell everything from comic strips and crossword puzzles to columns covering nearly all areas of human interest, such as politics, health, home maintenance, food, interpersonal relationships, etiquette, and general advice. A single columnist may be printed in hundreds of newspapers as a result of syndication. A popular comic strip like "Peanuts" may reach newspapers all over the world through the syndicate.

There are also picture syndicates, some of them adjuncts of other organizations, like the Associated Press Wide World; others are independent suppliers of photographs coming from many sources. The AP pioneered in the transmission of pictures by wire, now a regular feature in the newsrooms of large papers.

GROUP JOURNALS

In terms of business organization, the most striking development of this century has been the spread of what was once known as chain journalism. The owners now prefer to call them "groups" or "multiple ownerships," to avoid criticism of them as monoliths or monopolies.

Group journalism is increasing in the United States because of rising costs in newspaper operation; obviously, it is more economical to spread those costs over several newspapers. Even competing newspapers in some cities—San Francisco, for example—have found it a financial lifesaver to combine some of their business operations but retain the independence of the editorial and advertising departments. To those who see increasing monopoly in all these developments, newspaper owners point out that the alternative is fewer newspapers as individual journals succumb to cost factors.

SMALL-TOWN WEEKLIES AND DAILIES

There is one striking difference between working for a small-town weekly or daily and being on the staff of a large metropolitan paper, quite aside from the obvious difference in size. The big-city reporter goes out on an assignment, covers the story, and presumably will not again see the people who made the news unless they are public officials. By contrast, the small-town newspaper reporter not only sees the same people repeatedly, perhaps several times a week, but may also see them socially and will certainly see them in restaurants and bars, in church, at sports events, or on the street. It's the difference between big-city anonymity and small-town togetherness.

Inevitably, this primary difference has an effect on the work of the reporter—and for that matter, on the way the editor runs the paper. Small-town editors often like to proclaim their independence, but few of them make it stick. They are totally dependent on local merchants for advertising and, in some cases, on local bankers for financing. An ardently liberal Democratic editor, for instance, who comes into a solidly conservative Republican community and begins crusading for left-of-center causes may well be in serious trouble. Organized businesspeople in such a town can just about dictate what kind of local paper they will have.

WORKING ON SMALLER-CITY DAILIES

What is the difference between a small-town daily and a smaller-city daily? Or between a small-town weekly and daily aside from frequency of publication?

Fair questions, but not easy to answer. When a small-town weekly in a community of five thousand, let's say, turns itself into a daily, usually as population increases, certain changes take place. A wire service printer is installed to bring domestic and foreign news not previously carried, and more syndicated material is contracted. This quite often is political columns, because the paper will now more closely resemble its big-city neighbors and lose some of its local flavor and bulletin-board character. More staff will no doubt be added, both in the editorial and composing areas, simply because the effort required to put out five editions a week takes more people. Adding reporters and editors means that the original staff will not have to cover so much territory individually.

But a small-town daily is not transformed into a small-city daily simply because a community with a population of somewhere between twenty-five thousand and seventy-five thousand is large enough to demand a news organization modeled much more closely on the metropolitan daily.

The distinctions between the two are unavoidably blurred, and there is a great deal of overlapping. Some small-town dailies are so beautifully written and edited that they compare favorably with papers in cities of more than a million population, even though they do not carry as many pages. On the other hand, there are papers in some of the largest "small cities" that are journalistic junk piles and would hardly do credit to any community of any size.

LIFE ON THE BIG-CITY NEWSPAPERS

The Illusion

It's always been hard to explain life on metropolitan dailies to people whose only source of information about them has been motion pictures, the theater, and perhaps a few books. Until *All the President's Men* was made, generations of Americans formed their impression of big city newspaper life from that perennial play and motion picture, *The Front Page*, and its many imitators.

The image presented by these productions was a city room bordering on chaos, with city editors yelling "Copyboy!" at the top of their lungs and thrusting their tough jaws at cocky young reporters, saying, "Now go out and get that story and don't come back here without it." The city editor was customarily depicted as a tough/tender tyrant devoting all his time to breaking up sinister combinations of gangsters and politicians, while his reporters were shown to us as brash, fast-talking young men who spent their days tracking down criminals and breaking up gangs when they weren't drinking themselves to death.

The Reality

In reality, newspapers are simply organizations devised to gather the news of what is happening in the community, state, nation, and world. Editors and publishers certainly have political views, which they advance legitimately in the editorial columns, but their chief concerns are to keep the paper viable economically and ideally to get all the news they can, whatever it may be, without fear or favor. The reporters, as we've seen, don't wander aimlessly about looking for news, but are sent to where it is happening, has just happened, or may happen.

Most metropolitan papers, though they cover national and foreign news to varying extents, are more interested in city hall and police headquarters. Since space for news is always limited, the inclination is to condense world and national news as much as possible, except for presidential happenings and congressional doings with local implications.

Following are the top one hundred daily newspapers in the United States.

Top Newspapers by Circulation

The top one-hundred list of newspapers is based upon Audit Bureau of Circulation reports for the six-month period ending September 30, 1998. The final audit numbers were released in February 1999 and compiled for the *1999 Editor & Publisher International Year Book*. The list was published in May 1999.

UNITED STATES–DAILY

City	Newspaper	Circulation
New York (NY)	*Wall Street Journal*	1,740,450
Arlington (VA)	*USA Today*	1,653,428
Los Angeles (CA)	*Times*	1,067,540
New York (NY)	*Times*	1,066,658
Washington (DC)	*Post*	759,122
New York (NY)	*Daily News*	723,143
Chicago (IL)	*Tribune*	673,508
Long Island (NY)	*Newsday*	572,444
Houston (TX)	*Chronicle*	550,763
Chicago (IL)	*Sun-Times*	485,666
Dallas (TX)	*Morning News*	479,863
San Francisco (CA)	*Chronicle*	475,324
Boston (MA)	*Globe*	470,825
New York (NY)	*Post*	437,467
Phoenix (AZ)	*Arizona Republic*	435,330
Philadelphia (PA)	*Inquirer*	428,895
Newark (NJ)	*Star-Ledger*	407,026
Cleveland (OH)	*Plain Dealer*	382,933
Detroit (MI)	*Free Press*	378,256
San Diego (CA)	*Union-Tribune*	378,112
Orange County (CA)	*Register*	356,953
Miami (FL)	*Herald*	349,114
Portland (OR)	*Oregonian*	346,593
St. Petersburg (FL)	*Times*	344,784
Denver (CO)	*Post*	341,554
Minneapolis (MN)	*Star Tribune*	334,751
Denver (CO)	*Rocky Mountain News*	331,978
St. Louis (MO)	*Post-Dispatch*	329,582
Baltimore (MD)	*Sun*	314,033
Atlanta (GA)	*Constitution*	303,698
San Jose (CA)	*Mercury News*	290,885
Milwaukee (WI)	*Journal Sentinel*	285,776

City	Newspaper	Circulation
Sacramento (CA)	*Bee*	283,589
Kansas City (MO)	*Star*	281,596
Boston (MA)	*Herald*	271,425
New Orleans (LA)	*Times-Picayune*	259,317
Fort Lauderdale (FL)	*Sun-Sentinel*	258,726
Orlando (FL)	*Sentinel*	258,726
Los Angeles (CA)	*Investor's Business Daily*	251,172
Columbus (OH)	*Dispatch*	246,528
Detroit (MI)	*News*	245,351
Charlotte (NC)	*Observer*	243,818
Pittsburgh (PA)	*Post-Gazette*	243,453
Buffalo (NY)	*News*	237,229
Tampa (FL)	*Tribune*	235,786
Fort Worth (TX)	*Star-Telegram*	232,112
Indianapolis (IN)	*Star*	230,223
Louisville (KY)	*Courier-Journal*	228,144
Seattle (WA)	*Times*	227,715
Omaha (NE)	*World-Herald*	219,891
San Antonio (TX)	*Express-News*	218,661
Hartford (CT)	*Courant*	211,041
Richmond (VA)	*Times-Dispatch*	207,175
Oklahoma City (OK)	*Daily Oklahoman*	204,963
Los Angeles (CA)	*Daily News*	201,107
St. Paul (MN)	*Pioneer Press*	199,119
Norfolk (VA)	*Virginian-Pilot*	197,773
Seattle (WA)	*Post-Intelligencer*	196,271
Cincinnati (OH)	*Enquirer*	196,181
Nashville (TN)	*Tennessean*	184,979
Austin (TX)	*American-Statesman*	183,319
Philadelphia (PA)	*Daily News*	175,448
Rochester (NY)	*Democrat and Chronicle*	174,579
Little Rock (AR)	*Democrat-Gazette*	173,316
West Palm Beach (FL)	*Palm Beach Post*	173,074
Jacksonville (FL)	*Times-Union*	172,511
Providence (RI)	*Journal*	167,381
Memphis (TN)	*Commercial Appeal*	163,603
Des Moines (IA)	*Register*	163,292
Tulsa (OK)	*World*	162,186
Riverside (CA)	*Press-Enterprise*	161,612
Neptune (NJ)	*Asbury Park Press*	159,472
Raleigh (NC)	*News & Observer*	157,634
Fresno (CA)	*Bee*	155,931
Dayton (OH)	*Daily News*	152,308
White Plains (NY)	*Journal News*	151,695
Las Vegas (NV)	*Review-Journal*	151,162
Birmingham (AL)	*News*	148,835
Toledo (OH)	*Blade*	146,138

City	Newspaper	Circulation
Akron (OH)	*Beacon Journal*	143,199
Bergen County (NJ)	*Record*	141,368
Arlington Heights (IL)	*Daily Herald*	141,703
Grand Rapids (MI)	*Press*	139,703
Salt Lake City (UT)	*Tribune*	129,612
Allentown (PA)	*Morning Call*	129,522
Tacoma (WA)	*News Tribune*	129,247
Wilmington (DE)	*News Journal*	125,401
Columbia (SC)	*State*	120,433
Knoxville (TN)	*News-Sentinel*	115,248
Spokane (WA)	*Spokesman-Review*	114,475
San Francisco (CA)	*Examiner*	113,198
Lexington (KY)	*Herald-Leader*	113,036
Albuquerque (NM)	*Journal*	112,751
Sarasota (FL)	*Herald-Tribune*	109,438
Charleston (SC)	*Post & Courier*	109,272
Atlanta (GA)	*Journal*	106,896
Worcester (MA)	*Telegram & Gazette*	105,896
Jackson (MS)	*Clarion-Ledger*	105,382
Long Beach (CA)	*Press-Telegram*	105,167
Honolulu (HI)	*Advertiser*	102,358

CANADA–TOP TEN DAILY NEWSPAPERS

Toronto (ON)	*Star*	460,654
Toronto (ON)	*National Post*	325,000
Toronto (ON)	*Globe and Mail*	309,046
Montreal (QC)	*Le Journal*	254,957
Toronto (ON)	*Sun*	240,164
Vancouver (BC)	*Sun*	189,823
Montreal (QC)	*La Presse*	168,881
Vancouver (BC)	*Province*	156,688
Montreal (QC)	*Gazette*	141,595
Edmonton (AB)	*Journal*	141,583

Beat Reporters

The average metropolitan daily's city staff is the vital center of the paper, and covering the city hall and police beats may well be the most interesting part of it. These reporters become specialists if they stay on the beat long enough, and some are so happy doing this kind of work that they are unhappy if they are promoted to a city room job.

This will not seem comprehensible to many beginners who find themselves assigned to that beat on their first job—as so many are, since it is traditional to break in new reporters there on all but the largest papers. (Many dailies have a policy of circulating new reporters around on all the beats at the beginning to see if they have any special talents and to give them a feel for the paper's whole news operation.) But to young reporters covering their first metropolitan police beat, it may seem that they have been sent to Siberia. Pressrooms in police headquarters are notoriously and historically places where anyone who was not being paid for it would not want to spend any time. Small, usually dirty, and devoid of human comforts, the beats can also be lonely places in towns with only one newspaper.

Bureau Reporters

In addition to beat work on newspapers, there are also the bureaus, wherever they may be. At the bottom of the pecking order are the bureaus that may be maintained in other cities of a state. One is certain to be in the state capital, if that is not in a major city, and there the job is legislative and court reporting.

Otherwise, work in a bureau is much like working on a newspaper, except that the staff is small and general assignments are the rule. The specialists are mostly in New York City and Washington, DC. Bureau reporters cover local stories of sufficient general interest to go out on the wire. They also rewrite stories that appear in the local paper, or papers, that have the same general interest. There is nothing clandestine about this, of course. If a bureau isn't large enough to have its own quarters, it will probably be housed in or near the city room of a member or client newspaper, and the interchange is made freely since the newsgathering is cooperative. The AP and UPI are in competition with each other, not with the papers they serve.

It is the bureau chief's job to see that the city, state, or region for which he or she is responsible is covered thoroughly and the stories put on the wire to New York or Washington as rapidly as possible. The bureau chief is also on the receiving end of inquiries from headquarters, which may originate from the editors there or may be a query emanating from a member or client. The queries ask for more information on a story already transmitted or request the bureau to check on a report involving a particular area. The bureau chief's job is a busy one that may be a stepping-stone for advancement within the organization or to executive jobs on newspapers.

State bureaus are linked to the newspaper through the state desk in the newsroom, where the state editor handles not only the copy from the bureaus but also what is mailed or telephoned in by stringers. No matter in what part of this system a reporter labors, it is parochial work, like being on a small-town paper, and it is usually considered a step to better things.

Other Specialties

What are the better things? That depends on the interests of the reporter, but generally speaking, the opportunity to work exclusively in a field that is considered constantly absorbing and exciting is a better thing. Labor reporting, for example, can be a rewarding field these days, and these specialists will never be able to complain of having nothing to do.

Some reporters find that their particular talent is feature writing, and they wind up covering the news of the city that was once called "human interest"— that is, stories involving the daily life of humanity that isn't spot news. Feature writers usually are experts in interviewing, and they get assignments to interview visiting celebrities of every kind. Reporters who do this kind of work are often the incipient book and magazine writers on the staff.

An important part of the metropolitan daily is the section on business and financial news. This part of the paper has experienced expansion in recent years, and people with strong knowledge of economics, finance, the stock market, and other business-related topics may be assigned to the business section. Young reporters with an interest in these matters will find themselves in much more demand than those whose interests are more general, and they will discover a good many absorbing things to occupy their time.

The other daily specialties on the paper, as distinct from Sunday staff, would include sports, often an almost autonomous department; the arts, to which few metropolitan dailies devote much daily space except for motion pictures; and what used to be known as the women's pages, which today are more likely to be called by some euphemistic title like "Life-Style" or "Family Living."

EDITORIAL POSITIONS

Thus far, this chapter has explored the variety of jobs for beginning reporters at big-city daily newspapers. There are, of course, higher levels of responsibility to which the novice may aspire. Metropolitan dailies have a wide array of editors responsible for the individual sections of the paper, such as city editor, suburban editor, sports editor, arts editor, business editor, and others. Each of these people may have one or more assistant editors. There are also numerous copy editors and their assistants.

The upper echelons include the news editor, managing editor, executive editor, and publisher. People in these positions usually have spent their lives in the newspaper business and achieve such responsibility only after many years of hard work.

WORKING FOR THE WIRE SERVICES

Oldest of the two major American wire services is the Associated Press (AP), dating to 1848 in its embryonic form, existing as eastern and western divisions during the latter part of the nineteenth century, and emerging in this century as a worldwide cooperative enterprise. The structure of the AP is like that of a club. A newspaper has to be elected to membership by the other members and is granted a franchise. Because there are restrictions that somewhat guarantee the value of the franchise, it has a definite value as a tangible asset and can be sold like any piece of real property, although only with the approval of the AP membership.

The United Press International (UPI), on the other hand, is a service for sale to anyone who will pay the price. It was begun in 1907 by E. W. Scripps, who founded the Scripps-Howard newspapers. Scripps, whose ideas at the time were more populist than those of his fellow publishers, disliked the exclusivity of the AP franchise system. Believing that any publisher who wanted one should have a wire service, he began what was to become the United Press. Two years later, in 1909, William Randolph Hearst inaugurated his International News Service (INS), an outgrowth of the leased wire services that already linked his newspaper chain. After a sometimes gaudy career, during which it distinguished itself largely in its foreign correspondence, INS was merged with the United Press in 1958, as part of the reorganization of Hearst's declining empire, to form United Press International.

Both agencies have their headquarters on the East Coast, the AP in its own building in Rockefeller Center in New York City and the UPI in Washington, DC. News flows in from the world to these headquarters and goes out again on several different systems to members and clients. Both agencies also have picture and feature divisions that distribute everything from news photos to comic strips.

The agencies also have large Washington staffs covering the White House and Capitol Hill, including political columnists whose work goes out on the wire, too, serving especially the papers that do not have a Washington staff of their own. To compete with them, the *New York Times, Washington Post,* and *Los Angeles Times* syndicate the work of their Washington writers. Still other columnists are available to newspapers through independent syndicates.

The aim of many reporters who intend to stay in wire service work and who are laboring away in bureaus across the country, is to be transferred to New York, not only because it is at the center of operations, but also because it is the jumping-off point to assignment in Washington, DC, or in one of the foreign bureaus. Needless to say, these assignments are coveted by a good many people and not everyone who aspires to get one succeeds. But the wire services do encourage young talent, and those who do good work can hope for one of these prize assignments, if that is their goal.

Foreign Bureaus

The foreign bureaus operate in the same way as the domestic ones, covering the news of a capital city in the usual way and maintaining a system of stringers in other parts of the country. When major events occur requiring more help, reporters are assigned from other bureaus, either those nearby or from the well-staffed offices in London and Paris, where foreign operations are centered.

Transmission of news to the United States is done by cable and radiotelephone. Satellite transmission has been a major help in speeding up coverage, but the bulk of news still moves by cable in that esoteric language known as *cablese*, which foreign reporters must learn. Cablese is based on the elimination of articles and prepositions and the combining of words, all done for the purpose of saving money on cable costs.

Other Services

Between them, the AP and the UPI do an excellent job of covering the news of the world; however, since it is not humanly possible for the wire services to be everywhere, major newspapers often buy the services of national wire organizations in other countries. Oldest and best known of these is Reuters, the British service that began in 1851 and employed pigeons to carry messages before wires came into general use. Reuters is also a worldwide organization, based in London, with offices in major American cities. Another important foreign service is Agence France-Presse, the French service that was particularly useful to American papers during the Vietnam War because its correspondents were able to report from places like Hanoi, North Vietnam, where few American correspondents could penetrate. Agence France-Presse has been similarly useful in Asia and Africa at various times.

Some newspapers maintain foreign staffs today, but the great days of the *New York Herald Tribune* and *Chicago Daily News* correspondents have long since gone. Today the *New York Times, Los Angeles Times,* and *Washington Post* are the leaders, although the *Christian Science Monitor* (especially noted for its coverage) and *Baltimore Sun* also have foreign bureaus in the important capitals. A few have at least a European bureau, with perhaps a few floating correspondents elsewhere, notably the *Chicago Tribune, Minneapolis Tribune, Cleveland Plain Dealer, Toledo Blade, New York Daily News, San Francisco Chronicle,* and *Wall Street Journal.*

Viewed as a way of working life, wire services offer those entering the newspaper industry valuable experience in covering all kinds of news against constant time pressures, with, in the opinion of many, higher overall standards of accuracy than most newspapers maintain. Against the anonymity of the work, at least until a reporter rises to the New York, Washington, or foreign levels, must be balanced the mobility inherent in wire service organizations.

Not all wire service reporters, of course, get to travel around the world, or even beyond the bureau in which they work. In that case, the young reporters will have to decide whether they like this kind of work well enough to stay with it and take their chances, or whether to look for a job elsewhere in which they can use the experience gained.

SUNDAY AND WEEKEND EDITIONS

The Sunday newspaper in America is not what it used to be, but then, what is? Rising production costs have decreased the number of Sunday papers now published, and the competition of television and magazines has been felt in their advertising departments. Nevertheless, the Sunday newspaper, originated in the late 1800s by Joseph Pulitzer, continues to thrive in some cities. Even in such a leisure-oriented society as ours, where a dozen other things compete for attention on Sunday, the newspaper offers familiar relaxation before the day begins.

The average Sunday paper in America has become a more-or-less standardized product, although there are variations. The size of each one, of course, is determined by the amount of advertising the paper is able to obtain, and that appears to be limited mostly by the economic health of the city and the nation; competition from one or more local sources may also cut it down.

A Sunday newspaper sometimes begins with a colored comic section wrapped around the outside to give it visibility on the newsstand, even though that is no longer necessary in one-newspaper towns. Inside are the news sections, on Sunday carrying not only the spot news of that day but a variety of background and feature stories of a less timely nature. The comic section comes through a syndicate, and the news section is prepared in the newsroom. Everything else is in the domain of the Sunday editor, except for whatever syndicated magazine supplements the paper may buy, and with one other exception—sports.

Standard Sections

What the "everything else" encompasses depends on the kind of Sunday newspaper the management is trying to produce, but there are standard ingredients. One is a city or metro section, by whatever name it may be called, which will carry full-length local feature stories and possibly movie and theater news and advertising as well. In some cases, movie and theater information is included in an arts or entertainment section rather than the city section.

Another standard Sunday section is real estate, with few exceptions used chiefly as a promotion device for advertisers. This has been the case traditionally, but lately there have been papers that use this section to discuss urban problems, to talk about architecture, and to provide people with housing information.

Similar to the real estate section is the automobile section. It may contain a few articles about the latest models of cars and trucks, but most of its space is taken up by large display ads from auto dealers and smaller classified ads placed by people wishing to buy or sell vehicles.

Travel may well be a separate section, unless it is reduced to a few pages or columns in another section. Like real estate, it is most often used as a supplement to the advertising.

Women's traditional interests still receive a good deal of attention in the Sunday papers, but the packaging has changed in the wake of feminist influence throughout the 1970s and 1980s. Fewer papers have a blatantly titled "women's" section. Instead, there may be several sections catering to what were once considered primarily female concerns, such as food or fashion.

Some newspapers are creating a general "lifestyle" section to address the interests of an American population that no longer fits the traditional family image of husband, wife, and children. Topics covered may include health concerns and advice on such matters as divorce, single parenthood, interpersonal relationships, and career goals. Sometimes food and fashion are included in this section.

There is so much variation in the way Sunday financial sections are prepared that it's hard to generalize about them. Sometimes they are entirely the product of the staff that produces the daily financial pages, but if the paper is large enough, it may have an entire Sunday financial staff. In any case, it's a good bet that the daily writers will also be appearing on Sunday. Sunday staff writers are likely to do mostly background and summary stories about the week's financial events. Although these pages may be heavy with financial advertising, besides various market summaries, there is seldom any collusion with advertisers as there is in real estate and travel.

A few papers imitate the *New York Times's* famed "Week in Review" section. This Sunday feature carries the editorial and Op-Ed page seen every day and summarizes the news in short, signed background pieces broken down into categories.

The sports section appears much as it would on any other day, but it may have more background pieces and may also include a page on boating, photography, or some other sports-related hobby. The problem with Sunday sports sections is that they usually close too early to get a great deal of the important spot news in, and so they must depend heavily on stories written before events and on background stories.

If the paper has a separate arts or entertainment section, the average effort in this direction is not much to inspire enthusiasm. Advertising will be heavy, and around it will appear a few local reviews of movie or theater or music productions. There usually is also a great deal of material from public relations writers and press agents that has been edited slightly. Some papers, however, do make a serious effort to cover the cultural life of the community with reviews, features, pictures, interviews, and background stories about events such as theater, film, music, dance, visual arts, concerts, and special events. Done properly, these sections can be a great encouragement and help to local cultural organizations.

Weekend Editions

Some dailies try to take advantage of weekend advertising without going to the expense of a regular Sunday edition. The compromise is a so-called "weekend edition," which appears on Saturday morning (occasionally as late as the afternoon) and is intended to sell through the weekend, although most of the circulation is confined to Saturday.

The weekend edition is usually no more than a Saturday edition of the regular paper, considerably cut back in the news department, but often containing a large magazine insert. The insert has a variety of feature material, some produced by the paper's own staff but a great deal of it is likely to be syndicated. Weekend television listings will probably be carried, perhaps with accompanying stories or boxes that summarize what is being offered in movies or sports. Entertainment such as movies will be covered, bolstering the heavy advertising in that department. This may also be the occasion on which books are reviewed. The reviews may be staff-written or bought from a syndicate. An excellent book review column has been distributed by the AP for years and is used by many papers.

The weekend newspaper also may have huge advertising sections for such markets as real estate and automobiles, catering to Saturday shoppers. There may be some travel ads, since many travel agencies and tour operators are closed on Sundays.

Though the weekend edition is largely put out by the regular staff, it will probably have an editor or two in charge of it, offering further job opportunities closely related to Sunday department work. Most of these editors are likely to be working at other jobs on the paper as well.

CHAPTER 7

PREPARING FOR A NEWSPAPER CAREER

For those who plan a career in newspaper reporting and editorial work, a major decision they must make is what kind of education to pursue. At some point on the road to making this decision, students are almost certain to encounter the argument that on-the-job training is all they need and that it's a mistake to consider a journalism school or department.

This argument comes not only from older people in the profession (especially from those who still think it's a trade), but also from conservative academicians who regard journalism training as a vocational intrusion on the sanctity of liberal arts programs.

This opposition, from both sources, has begun to crumble. The sharp increase of vocationalism in general and the dramatic upward surge of journalism education enrollments in the past twenty-five years have combined to mute the academic attack, although the diehards persist. There are diehards in the newspaper business, too, but they are disappearing, simply because the schools and departments have now heavily populated the entire communications industry.

It is also important to remember, however, that formal journalism education is not necessarily essential to get a job in the business, nor to succeed in it. A great many writers and editors have had no such training, and it is possible to "learn on the job," provided someone will hire you and take the time to teach you. This, of course, assumes you understand basic spelling, grammar, and sentence structure. There are, too, individuals who have so much natural talent, they seem to know instinctively what to do and how to do it.

WHY STUDY JOURNALISM?

Why study journalism then? There are several good reasons. One is that it will save you a substantial amount of career time. Graduates of a good journalism school or department will have such a comprehensive background in the basic skills and so much specialized knowledge to go with it, that they will be able to take a newsroom job the day after they graduate.

Another reason for studying journalism is the opportunity it offers you to survey the career possibilities available in the whole area of communications. A good school or department will offer course sequences in newspaper work, magazine work, public relations, broadcast journalism, and, in a few places, advertising as well. Many offer undergraduate and graduate programs in communications theory, "the sociology of journalism," which has now become a virtual necessity for teaching in the field.

To cite still another reason for journalism study, if the work is done with skilled professionals who are still at work themselves, which is the case in the best schools, it is equivalent to a year's training in a newsroom, and in some ways better, because it is training not acquired by chance or by making mistakes that can get you fired. The work and atmosphere of a newsroom is created, offering many opportunities to meet and talk with working professionals to learn what is going on in the business.

A Case for a Communications Degree

Another viable route to a career in publishing is a degree in communications. Communications majors enter publishing as easily and as often as journalism majors.

Communications majors can plan ahead while in school, taking courses and honing skills that will allow them to work in any number of media outlets. While many of the skills needed are field-specific, just as many others can be transferred for use from one sector of the media to another. The value of a communications degree is widely recognized as the backbone of a myriad of fields.

SELECTING A SCHOOL

Your local library should have career guides that list the various colleges and universities that offer journalism and communications programs. Hundreds of programs are available.

Armed with guides, you, as a prospective journalism and communications student, should first decide what area of the country you want to study in—a decision that will, no doubt, be influenced by family and financial factors. If you can go anywhere, you will be free to choose from the best-known programs in large schools as well as from those offered in smaller institutions. In any case, you should zero in on three or four places that appeal most to you and where financial help is available if you need it. Give yourself some latitude, because there is always the possibility that you may not be accepted by your first choice, or even the second.

If it is at all possible, you should visit the institution itself, meet the dean or head if available, talk to professors and students, perhaps even ask to sit in on a class. There is no better way to get the "feel" of a school than by this process. By visualizing yourself in that setting, with these people, you can get at least some preliminary idea of whether you'll be happy there.

Participating in Internships

Internships help to not only prepare you for a career in publishing, but also to help you get a foot in the door when it comes time for the job hunt. Employers would rather hire someone they know, someone with a proven record.

Another successful method is to take more than the one required college internship. If you can get involved in two or even three internships, you'll make more contacts and have a better chance of lining up full-time employment when you graduate. At the same time you'll be adding to your portfolio and creating impressive specifics to include on your resume.

GRADUATE SCHOOL

After graduation you must make another decision: Should I go right to work or enter graduate school? Often, financial conditions will make that decision for you, without argument. But if graduate school is possible, the question is whether to go for a master's or a doctorate degree and whether it should be in a graduate journalism program or elsewhere.

For people who feel confident of the professional preparation they got in their undergraduate training and who have decided to go into a part of the communications business that requires a good deal of background, it may be wise to get a graduate degree in some field other than journalism. Political science, history, one of the sciences, even the law are all possibilities; others depend on particular interests and ambitions. If you choose the kind of specialization that graduate programs in journalism offer, a glance at the guides you have obtained will disclose the accredited programs for master's and doctoral candidates.

The primary difference among the graduate schools is the varying emphasis they place on specialized professional training beyond the undergraduate level, as opposed to communications research, which trains for teaching and research rather than writing and editing. One-year master's degree programs are likely to be professionally oriented; nearly all doctoral programs are directed toward research and teaching.

GETTING STARTED

Getting started as a reporter or editor in the newspaper business is seldom easy. Good times and bad, year in and year out, there always seem to be more talented, eager applicants than there are jobs. Yet there is always competition among employers for the best.

The communications industry has become so broad, and institutional programs so diverse to match these multiple needs, that the available talent pool splits itself up and not as many are as available to newspapers as in earlier days. Broadcasting claims a large number of graduates now, and so do the nation's thousands of magazines. Others go into advertising, and more are now discovering book publishing as that industry grows ever larger and ever more visible to the public eye.

EMPLOYMENT OUTLOOK

Through the year 2006, the outlook for most editing jobs is expected to continue to be competitive, because so many people are attracted to the field. Online publications and services, which are relatively new, will continue to grow and require an increased number of writers and editors. Opportunities should be better on small daily and weekly newspapers, where the pay is low, rather than with the larger dailies.

Some small publications are hiring freelance copy editors as backup for their staff editors, or for additional help with special projects.

Employment of editors is expected to increase faster than the average for all occupations through the year 2006. Employment of salaried editors by newspapers is expected to increase with growing demand for their publications.

Many job openings will also occur as experienced workers transfer to other occupations or leave the labor force. Turnover is relatively high in this occupation—many freelancers leave because they can not earn enough money.

FINDING A JOB

For the graduates facing these prospects who have concluded that no matter what happens, they must work on a newspaper of some kind, there are methods to employ in finding a job. Crass as it may sound, the best approach is to take advantage of any contact with people in the business—a relative, a friend, or a teacher. Nothing is better than a personal introduction and recommendation.

If no such entrée is available, the "shotgun" technique offers a tried and proven method used by many graduates. Get a copy of the annual directory of newspapers published by the trade magazine *Editor & Publisher*, and write to every possible name. The *Gale Directory of Publications* also gives an exhaustive listing of newspapers. Keep at it until your postage money and patience run out. It would be a rare thing if, out of several hundred letters, a job did not result. Also scan the local newspaper want ads for openings.

The only alternative to this method or the personal introduction is to walk in cold at the newspaper nearest you and ask for the personnel director or for the city editor or managing editor. Tell your story, trying to sell yourself. That may seem like a long shot, and it is, but jobs are secured in this fashion every day.

Your school may also be able to help you find a job. College placement centers can be a valuable resource in matching you to prospective employers visiting the campus or in alerting you to job openings not publicly advertised.

Resume and Stringbook

Whatever approach you take, you should have prepared a resume, which is essentially a list of your work experience, education, and other activities, with your name, address, and phone number at the top. The career guidance section of your library or bookstore should have a variety of books on resume writing if you need help in deciding what to put in yours. (Two good sources on writing resumes are published by VGM Career Books: *Resumes for Communications Careers* and *Resumes for College Students and Recent Graduates.*)

In addition to your resume, a stringbook is a valuable selling point for a beginning reporter. A stringbook is simply a collection of story clippings, probably from your school newspaper at first. Bring the stringbook with you to an interview in case a prospective employer wishes to view the scope of your work. When an advertised job opening requests clippings from applicants, you can select two or three of your best efforts to submit. Most employers will accept photocopies; avoid sending your only original if possible.

If you are responding in writing to a job opening, you will need to draft a cover letter to accompany your resume and possible clips. The cover letter should briefly state why you are interested in the particular job and perhaps point out one or two of your credentials that seem most valuable for it. (See *Cover Letters They Don't Forget,* published by VGM Career Books.) Do not simply repeat what is on your resume; the employer can read it.

After an interview, write a short letter thanking the employer for talking with you and reiterate your interest in the position—if you are indeed still interested.

SALARIES

Beginning salaries for editorial assistants, according to the Dow Jones Newspaper Fund, average $21,000 annually. According to the Newspaper Guild, those who have at least five years' experience average more than $30,000, and senior editors at the largest newspapers earn more than $67,000 a year.

The average annual salary for editors in the federal government in nonsupervisory, supervisory, and managerial positions is about $47,500; other editors average about $47,000.

The Newspaper Guild negotiates with individual newspapers on minimum salaries for both starting reporters and those still on the job after three to six years. The median minimum salary for reporters is about $550 a week. The median minimum weekly salary for reporters after three to six years on the job is about $850 a week.

CHAPTER 8

JOBS IN NEWSPAPER PUBLISHING

EDITORIAL

The editorial department of a newspaper is usually composed of two distinct subdepartments: news and editorial. The distinction is basic. The *news department* deals in fact; the *editorial department* deals in opinion. The two are kept separate for obvious reasons.

Also kept separate are the other departments necessary to publish a newspaper—the *advertising department,* the chief moneymaking arm of the newspaper; the *circulation department,* which distributes the newspaper and provides additional revenue; and the *production department,* which produces the newspaper. Although these are separate departments of a newspaper, they obviously have to work closely together.

Writers

Writers are needed in the news, features, sports, and editorial departments. Newswriters cover special events, do interviews, gather information, and prepare factual articles. Writers typically are given "beats" or are employed as "general assignment" reporters. A beat reporter can cover a geographical beat, such as a city, town, or country, or a topical beat, such as police, medicine, government, courts, or sports. Frequently, a reporter covering a geographical beat covers the government, courts, police, and so forth, within that area. A general assignment reporter is given assignments by an editor, as opposed to covering a beat and developing stories individually.

The pleasure of general assignment reporting is its infinite variety. To come to work not knowing whether you will be sent to cover a banquet for five hundred people with a prominent speaker, to interview a visiting celebrity who may be a movie star or a scientist, to cover a fast-breaking murder story, or to attend a convention—that is a satisfying kind of day for a reporter who loves newspaper work.

On the other hand, a certain amount of boredom can set in. There are dull news nights and days, along with the active ones. The general assignment reporter sits at his or her desk, literally waiting for something to happen. A conscientious city editor will find something for the reporter to do, however. Perhaps the reporter will be given some continuing story from a previous edition and asked to put a second-day lead on it. This means calling the people involved to find out if anything new has happened, then rewriting the first story to present the new developments.

Rewrite Work

General assignment reporters on these smaller papers also do the rewrite work that specialists do exclusively on metropolitan dailies. The telephone on a rewrite desk is equipped with headphones, and when the city editor says, "Police beat on number 2," the reporter puts on the headset, punches the proper button, and hears the voice of the beat reporter in police headquarters who gives the pertinent facts on a story. The rewrite reporter takes notes, asks to have names spelled if there is any doubt, asks other questions, and then writes the story after hanging up. Sometimes the beat reporter will have as many as four or five stories at a time, enough to keep a rewrite reporter busy for a while.

Rewrite is not the only device used by city editors to take up a general assignment reporter's spare time, however. Obituaries and funeral notices are done by reporters on papers too small to have an obituary editor, meaning most of them. It is a job never spoken of with enthusiasm by those who have to do it. Funeral notices are called in by the undertaker or by the family of the deceased. Material for an obituary is sometimes sent in by a family or it may require a telephone call to them from a reporter—not the easiest kind of call to make, although there always seems to be someone who is able to provide the needed information.

For public figures whose names make news even in death, newspapers carry proof sheets, typed background information sheets, or—in more modern offices—computer files on people, the exact number depending on the size of the paper. Sometimes there are files of clippings concerning the deceased. All this material is kept in the paper's archives, which are known in this country as "the morgue," appropriate enough for obituary writing, but actually intended to cover a newspaper's entire file of clippings and photographs. These are used as background material for any kind of story. Some newspapers have transferred their early back-issue files to microfiche and computers.

City Editors

Newsroom organization begins with the core operation centered in the city editor's desk. City editors, a legendary breed in themselves, are in direct charge of the news organization that covers the city news, from the beat reporters to the rewrite reporters, if any, and including the photographers. The city editor may have additional responsibilities, and, in any case, will probably need one or two assistants. The city editor's job is to direct the work of the reporters and photographers and to see that they meet the paper's deadlines.

Copy Editors

When the city editor has okayed a reporter's story, it goes to the copydesk. In the old days, the copydesk was a horseshoe-shaped affair presided over by the chief copy editor who sat at a desk on the open head of the horseshoe; this position was called "in the slot." The copy editors, ranged around the perimeter of the horseshoe, were said to be "on the rim." The chief copy editor's job was to route the copy from the city editor, from the telegraph editor handling domestic news (if there was one), and from the cable editor (again, if there was one), to the copy editors on the rim. Those copy editors would correct spelling and punctuation, if required; improve the language, if necessary; style it for the printer, as far as capital letters, paragraphing, and so forth were needed; and finally, write a headline for it in a style dictated by the chief copy editor. These days, copy editors work on their own computers at their own desks.

Editorial Direction

The overall direction of the editorial department is the responsibility of several executives, including the city editor and all assistants; the wire service editors; the news editor; and the managing editor. Not all smaller dailies have a news editor. Typically, there is a separate news editor when there are more editors of specific areas. For example, there may be a suburban editor and a foreign editor in addition to the city editor. In such a case, a news editor coordinates their activities. A news editor generally sits near the copy editors and is the liaison between all the workers in the city room or newsroom and the copydesk. The news editor controls the flow of news to the copydesk, sometimes eliminating a story that doesn't seem sufficiently important or requesting changes in it from the reporter or specialist who wrote it. In collaboration with the city editor, the news editor decides on the relative importance of each story, determining its position in the paper and the prominence of the headline to be written for it.

Over all these executives is the managing editor, who does not usually sit in the newsroom with the others, but often in an adjacent office that has easy access in and out. The managing editor has overall responsibility for each day's editions, making decisions on whether to print a controversial story, directing the coverage of important stories, deciding matters of policy (if a question raised needs to go no higher), and in general, supervising the work of everyone else. The hand of a really good managing editor is felt in every department. In addition, the managing editor serves as the liaison between the newsroom and its executives, and the top echelon, which would include the editor (also known as the executive editor or, less commonly, the editor-in-chief) and the publisher. Both these people are responsible to the paper's board of directors.

The noneditorial side of a newspaper includes a number of other departments, which are discussed below.

ADVERTISING

To most people, a career in newspapering means writing and editing, and the word *newsperson* quite often is equated with the word *reporter.* Beyond the newsroom, however, is a large domain that keeps the paper functioning as a business organization. No matter what a paper does in getting the news and displaying it, the viability of any newspaper is determined by the successful functioning of its business side.

Advertising is critical to the financial success of a newspaper. For most papers, ad sales generate the bulk of all revenue—more than subscription sales or any other source. On a small-town weekly, the advertising sales staff may consist of one person who meets face-to-face with local merchants to persuade them to promote their businesses. A major metropolitan daily may have over a hundred people in its advertising department, and they are likely to be specialists in one particular area of sales.

The three main kinds of advertising sales are:

1. classified
2. retail or local
3. national

Classified Advertising

Classified advertising is the bread-and-butter of a newspaper. Those long columns of fine print you see in the classified sections are the product of a hard-working group of people who not only process the ads that people want to place in the paper, but also solicit advertising that has to do with businesses and services. The soliciting often is accomplished by telephone, as is much of the ad taking. Newspapers usually have substations in various parts of a large metropolitan area where people come to place classifieds. The ad taker often must help the customer in phrasing the advertisement as briefly and clearly as possible.

Retail or Local Advertising

Retail or local display ads are located primarily outside the classified section. They are the most commonly seen ads in most newspapers, set at the bottom of each page, with news stories and photos around them. A successful display ad will grab the reader's attention before he or she turns to the next page. Retail ads are the offerings of local merchants—department stores, clothing stores, restaurants, independent banks, small grocery stores, specialty shops, and, in fact, the whole range of businesses. The people in this department work closely with the merchants, helping them write their ads and suggesting ideas. The newspaper sales representative wants to ensure repeat business from the advertiser.

National Advertising

National advertising involves the solicitation of ads from merchandisers who have countrywide distribution, like automobile companies, firms that manufacture appliances, chainstores, or food companies. The work in this part of the advertising department is different from retail or classified sales because the newspaper salesperson often will be working with an advertising agency, rather than directly with the company. The biggest companies usually have their own advertising department that operates like an agency. National advertisers often prepare their own ad copy and submit it in camera-ready form. The job of the newspaper salesperson is to convince the national advertiser that the paper meets the advertiser's needs in terms of target audience and sales goals.

Co-op Advertising

In recent years, co-op advertising has become more popular. Co-op advertising is a combination of national and retail advertising. For example, Goodyear may run a large display ad describing its new radial tire, and at the bottom of the ad is the name and address of the local store where the tire is sold. The local store must contribute a proportionate amount toward the cost of the ad, but the national company picks up the bulk of the tab.

Co-op advertising benefits both the national company and the local merchant because they share the cost while offering a product to a specific market. Newspaper salespeople like co-op advertising because it can enable a local merchant who might not otherwise be able to afford it to place a significant ad in the paper.

CIRCULATION

Circulation essentially involves two things: getting the newspaper to its customers after it's printed, and dealing with the vendors who distribute it. The work of the circulation department begins when the folded papers roll off the presses into the mailing department, where they are wrapped in bundles, tied with wire, and loaded onto the fleet of trucks waiting for them. Some of these trucks service the city's newsstands, which may be on street corners, in stores, at airports, at bus and rail terminals, and in all kinds of retail establishments where newspapers are sold. Other bundles of papers go to distributors who service the paper's circulation zone; their customers are the local drugstores, hotels, and stores where newspapers are bought by the public. Some distributors also work with carriers who deliver papers door-to-door.

Circulation is concerned, then, with the physical means of distribution, which means a fleet of trucks for the city and other vehicles to supply the out-of-town distributors. That puts the circulation department in the transportation business. Since all these dealers, except those who are the distributor's customers, are clients of the paper, there is a great deal of paperwork involved in dealing with them.

Divisions

The circulation department of a daily newspaper is typically divided into a number of areas of responsibility. These include the following:

Distribution center production. This area includes assembling, counting, and bundling the papers as they come off the presses.

Transportation. This includes a fleet of trucks that deliver the bundled papers to their distribution points. A large newspaper may have several hundred vehicles in its fleet and employ mechanics as well as drivers.

Home delivery. People employed in this area receive the bundled papers from the truck and then distribute them to single-family homes using carriers. The carriers may be employed directly by the paper or operate as independent contractors.

Single-copy sales.   Like those in home delivery, people employed in this area receive the bundled papers from the truck, but their distribution is to vending machines and to dealers in retail establishments.

Subscription sales and service.   People in this area usually do their work over the phone. Some newspapers call their subscription sales division "telemarketing" as a result. Subscriber service representatives handle a variety of situations, most commonly calls from subscribers whose paper was not delivered.

PROMOTION

The promotion department is an important element in the noneditorial side of a newspaper. A newspaper must promote itself to several audiences: to the public at large (its potential customers); to special audiences within that public; and to potential advertisers. The most visible evidence of its work is the kind of outdoor advertising of the paper that appears on its own delivery trucks. As newspaper vans move about the city, their sides often are plastered with posters advertising some current feature in the newspaper—a column, a comic strip, an investigative report of some kind.

The Department's Work

But that is only the beginning of the promotion department's work. Its posters, streamers, and other devices to publicize something in the paper can be seen on newsstands, billboards, and at the retail distribution points. Some papers are using radio and television commercials to advertise their merits and get new readers. Some newspapers also send promotion staff to local schools to encourage use of the newspaper in the classroom.

To reach special audiences, the promotion department organizes community contests of various kinds, sets up a booth at a trade show or convention, or sponsors activities in a particular part of the city where it hopes to get increased circulation. All that is in addition to large citywide promotions, like the sponsoring of major athletic and other events. The promotion department uses leaflets, brochures, and other printed material to get the newspaper into the public consciousness.

PHOTOGRAPHY AND DESIGN

Photography and design are closely allied with the editorial side, yet they are not concerned with writing and editing. These are areas in which the artistically inclined can join the newspaper publishing business.

Today news photography is a wide-ranging field, producing, with sophisticated modern equipment, pictures that are not only newsworthy but also artistic accomplishments as well. Some news photographers have gone on to become well-known artists in their field. On many smaller papers, reporters have to take the pictures as well as write, and that ability is a hiring prerequisite. Larger papers have their own photography departments, with a director, technical facilities ranging all the way from adequate to elaborate, and a corps of highly skilled professionals who take the pictures. Often photographers and reporters work together as a team, going out on stories in a staff car. The common procedure on a breaking story is for the reporter, on getting an assignment from the city desk, to go to the photography department, where a photographer is assigned.

Photography Job Qualifications and Salaries

A newspaper photographer's job requires speed, creativity, persistence, stamina, and a good sense of timing. News photographers have always been a breed apart, often brash and outspoken, feeling a sense of camaraderie with one another, yet keenly competitive. Newspaper work is a particular kind of photography that appeals to a particular kind of photographer.

Many entry-level photography jobs do not require formal education. However, the photographer should have a basic understanding of photographic technique and darkroom work. Experience at a college newspaper can strengthen a photographer's portfolio and offer the experience that may provide an edge over other applicants in metropolitan markets, which are highly competitive.

The median annual earnings for salaried photographers and camera operators who worked full-time were about $30,000 in 1996. The middle 50 percent earned between $21,000 and $46,500. The top 10 percent earned more than $75,100, while the lowest 10 percent earned less than $14,500.[1]

Design

Journalistic design is a relatively new field in newspaper publishing. Today many papers are increasing their use of charts, diagrams, and maps, and newspaper

---

[1]*Occupational Outlook Handbook,* 1999.

art departments are expanding as a result. There are several areas of specialization in an art or design department, including:

Art production.   Cropping or retouching photographs, cutting silhouettes, and preparing final pieces of art are among the activities in this area.

Maps and charts.   News stories concerning world events are increasingly being accompanied by maps showing where the event occurred.

Graphics.   This area includes diagrams to accompany stories about science, medicine, or complex technical subjects. Bar graphs and pie charts are other examples of graphics.

Artistic and graphic designers work under the supervision of art directors, who coordinate their activities with those of the editors and photographers.

Median weekly earnings of experienced full-time designers were $590 in 1996. The middle 50 percent earned between $380 and $890, the bottom 10 percent earned less than $280, and the top 10 percent earned more than $1,300.[2]

PRODUCTION

Production involves the mechanics of getting the newspaper typeset and printed. This area has probably undergone the greatest amount of change as a result of recent technological developments.

Today's production department has two main parts, the composing room and the pressroom. Each of these two main areas may be further subdivided, depending on the size of the paper. The composing room is where the stories, photos, and ads are put together onto pages. The pressroom, of course, is where the paper is printed. Press operators set up and adjust the printing plates, make sure the paper and ink meet specifications, and adjust the flow of ink for even distribution across the page. Web-fed rotary presses are still most commonly used.

Today, most newspapers use computers in their newswriting and typesetting operations. Many of the major metropolitan dailies are well advanced toward automating their composing rooms. Smaller papers, using offset equipment, have also come a long way down this path. High equipment costs are still a barrier to some papers, but inevitably the prices will come down.

---

[2]*Ibid.*

New Equipment

Now the technological march is advancing on the newsroom, and the newspapers able to afford it are already using advanced equipment. The reporter typing out a story on a computer keyboard in Kansas City knows that the words are going to be transmitted directly to a central processing unit (CPU) that will decode the story and cause it to emerge on an editing screen in the home office. There it will be edited with an electronic pencil, after which it will be transferred to an automatic typesetting machine. In the newsroom, reporters' stories are typed into computers, from which they are transmitted into the CPU and can be called up again by the copy editor. Another method used to place material into the CPU is through an optical character reader (OCR), a device that "scans" a typewritten page and deposits a perfect copy of it into the CPU. Computers may use paper tape, magnetic tape, or direct electronic signals to transfer the edited stories into the typesetting machine.

COMPOSITION

Another area in which computers are gaining widespread use is in composition. In 1980 a company called Page Pro introduced the first computerized page layout system capable of full-scale pagination, meaning the placement of both text and photos in a page layout made on the computer. The traditional system of page makeup is a two-step process involving hand pasteup of typeset copy onto a layout sheet, with spaces left for photos, then integrating the text and photos onto a single piece of film from which the printing plate is made. With computerized pagination, the complete page is transferred directly from the video terminal to the typesetter, thus eliminating the composing room. However, page design on the computer can be more time-consuming than manual pasteup of pages.

PHOTOGRAPHY

The digital camera is revolutionizing photography. The camera is attached to a microcomputer, and when the photographer snaps a picture, the microcomputer converts the image into digital language for transmission to the office CPU via telephone or radio, completely bypassing the stage of film that has to be developed.

PRODUCTION

Even the printing process itself is being affected by new technology. The new ink-jet press eliminates the need for a metal printing plate as a computer controls the opening and closing of thousands of tiny nozzles that squirt jets of ink directly onto the paper to form the images. This type of press is not yet in wide use but could be someday. In the future, newsprint may also undergo a slight alteration. A fiber called *kenaf,* which is much like hemp, can be mixed with wood pulp to make newsprint. Kenaf would thus help alleviate the demand for wood pulp that is growing faster than the nation's supply of trees. Kenaf grows quickly, requires minimal care, and could be cultivated in most regions of the United States.

BUSINESS SUPPORT FUNCTIONS

A newspaper is first and foremost a business. Its success depends not only upon the work of those directly involved in the production and distribution of the paper, but also upon a support network of people who keep it functioning as a business.

Financial

The financial department is usually the largest of the business support functions. Its divisions include the following:

Accounting and bookkeeping.   Accurate records of the newspaper's receipts and expenditures are crucial for its continued success. Accountants should be college graduates who have passed the CPA (certified public accountant) exam. A college degree is not always required for bookkeepers, but some training or experience beyond high school is helpful.

Credit, billing, and collection.   People in this area are responsible for authorizing credit for qualified customers and advertisers, generating accurate invoices of payments due from them, and making sure that they pay their bills. Educational requirements for these jobs vary, but math ability and attention to detail are essential.

Accounts payable and payroll.   Neither creditors nor employees like to be kept waiting for their money, so this area is an important one. As with the previous area, educational requirements vary, but people seeking positions in this area should have a good grasp of math and be attentive to detail.

Customer service.   Though people in this area do not generally handle financial matters directly, they nevertheless play an important role in maintaining a positive public image of the paper. They are the unsung heroes who listen to complaints from customers, advertisers, or the general public and try to make sure that problems are resolved. The newspaper stands to lose revenue and goodwill without effective customer service. A college degree often is not required for employment in this area, but key personality traits include patience, listening skills, a desire to help other people, and the ability to think analytically in solving problems.

Planning.   People in this area look beyond today's financial picture and try to predict what will happen three to five years down the road. They set up future budgets and devise strategies concerning such topics as pricing, promotion, plant capacity, and the financial impact of new technological changes. These are not entry-level positions, but exemplary service in another area of the financial department can put one in line for such jobs.

Legal

Depending upon its size, a newspaper may hire a law firm on a retainer basis or may have a full-time legal staff. In special cases, as when a constitutional matter must be decided, an outside expert may be retained. The movie version of the newspaper lawyer depicts a person spending time and energy on libel actions, but in reality there are relatively few libel suits filed against newspapers, in part because one aspect of the lawyers' job is to prevent the paper from printing anything libelous in the first place. A newspaper lawyer is much more likely to be working on union problems or on the same kind of corporate law that would be practiced with any other large business.

Obviously, anyone who wants to work as a newspaper lawyer should have a law degree. There may be a few related assistant or clerical positions available that would not require a degree.

Human Resources

This department, also called personnel, is mainly concerned with the employees of the newspaper. A great deal of recordkeeping is involved at a large newspaper in terms of staff. Personnel must stay up-to-date on who is working for the company, in which department, at what salary, and with what benefits. This department calculates the paychecks, with deductions for insurance, pension plan contributions, taxes, Social Security, and any unpaid time off. It keeps track of vacation time allotted and used and sick days taken. Employees who violate company policy often are notified by the personnel manager.

However, aside from these day-to-day matters, the human resources department tries to determine how best to balance employee satisfaction with the company's inevitable financial constraints. Morale problems can affect the productivity of the organization and cannot be lightly dismissed. Employees need to feel that their services are valued and that they are receiving adequate compensation, not only in terms of money, but also in terms of benefits. Adequate health insurance, reasonable vacation time, and some provision for future financial security—a pension plan, profit-sharing, or the like—are among the benefits of chief concern to employees.

Traditionally, the personnel department was staffed by individuals who moved up from the secretarial pool or were transferred from another department. Today, with more emphasis being placed on human resource management, the department may be looking for someone with a college degree in business management, personnel, or even psychology. Courses in human behavior and organizational structure are an important supplement to regular business courses in economics, accounting, math, and marketing. Good interpersonal skills and strong writing and speaking ability are also a plus.

Clerical

The clerical staff includes secretaries, receptionists, and all those other variously labeled people who do the typing, filing, digging, and errand running that keep the business going. Clerical staff are among the lowest-paid employees in the business, yet it could not survive long without them.

Most clerical positions do not require formal education beyond high school, but there may be requirements for specific skills such as typing and computing. As business machinery becomes increasingly complex and computers become more widely used for even the most basic tasks, additional training at a vocational or technical school is recommended. Sometimes college graduates take a clerical position just to get a "foot in the door," but the job may be tougher than they expected. Helpful personal attributes for clerical jobs include patience, the ability to juggle several assignments at once, good organizational skills, the ability to get along with a variety of people, and a general tolerance for chaos.

Salaries for people employed in the business support functions of a newspaper will be comparable to those for the same kinds of jobs in other companies of similar size in the same geographic area. As a word of caution, it should be mentioned that there usually is not a great deal of movement from noneditorial areas of the paper into the editorial side. If what you really want to be is a reporter or editor, that is the position you should strive for from the outset.

PART THREE

MAGAZINE PUBLISHING

CHAPTER 9

THE MAGAZINE SCENE

Magazines—for almost all of us, they are a vital part of our daily lives. We've grown up with with one magazine or another; we see people browsing, buying, or reading magazines everywhere; and there is no limit to the choices available.

The first thing to remember about magazines is that they are available everywhere; they are widely distributed and capable of serving all sorts of people's interests, exceeding books and all other media in sheer quantity and readership. Only television viewing can possibly surpass magazine reading in popularity—but even there, it is widely held that television stimulates interest in subjects that will lead people to "read more about it" in books and magazines.

Then, magazines are *various*. Of all the print media, they offer by far the broadest range of human expression in text and pictures. Like books, they cover the globe, embracing every human activity and interest. Physically, magazines are composed of type and illustrations in color or black and white; but in actuality they are made up of entertainment, instruction, information, ideas, and advertising that often complements the editorial environment and the interests of the reader.

Magazines do have certain similarities to other media. In addition to informing and entertaining people, they often attempt to mold public opinion, and they assist the business community in showcasing its many products and services—as they pay their way—through advertising. Magazines can give a perspective to the news that a daily newspaper does not provide. Unlike television, magazines have to be read, and reading is active. Magazines can be carried anywhere you wish, from room to room or in a briefcase. They can be read and re-read as often as you like.

Finally, there are untold numbers of magazines. Nobody knows for sure quite how many different magazines exist. The Magazine Publishers Association, citing the *Gale Directory of Periodicals,* recognizes 13,139 American magazines (see table), but the 1999 edition of *The Standard Periodical Directory* lists 85,000 periodicals in the United States and Canada (most of them American). *The Standard Periodical Directory* is revised every two years; in one recent two-year period, there were some 11,000 new listings and 9,000 deletions—which gives you some idea of the dynamic, everchanging nature of the field of magazine publishing.

Number of Magazines by Category

Publication category	U.S.	Canada	Total
General circulation	2,933	307	3,240
Trade, technical, and professional publications	8,482	675	9,157
Agricultural publications	430	59	489
Black publications	53	0	53
College publications	224	21	245
Foreign language publications	168	194	362
Fraternal publications	64	3	67
Hispanic publications	67	0	67
Jewish publications	45	3	48
Religious publications	480	51	531
Women's publications	193	19	212
Total	13,139	1,332	14,471

A more commonly quoted figure for magazines in America—that is, for publications readily identifiable as magazines—is 22,000, give or take a thousand or two. Part of the problem comes in defining a magazine. The *Random House Dictionary of the English Language* defines it as "a publication that is issued periodically, usually bound in a paper cover, and typically containing stories, essays, poems, etc., by many writers, and often photographs and drawings, frequently specializing in a particular subject or area, as hobbies, news or sports." The word *magazine* comes to us from France, where one of the world's first magazines, called *Journal des Scavans,* was first published in Paris in 1655. A magazine was a storehouse for anything from dairy products to ammunition. Sometime during the eighteenth century it took on its present meaning.

It would be accurate to say that most magazines specialize in a particular subject or area, since only a small proportion of the total number are intended for a general audience. Magazines are difficult to categorize. *Standard Rate and Data Service (SRDS),* the directory most frequently used by advertisers and advertising agencies, contains fifty-one different categories of general magazines, ranging from advertising to metropolitan to woodworking, and twelve categories of farm publications, in classifications such as crops, chemicals, livestock, and poultry. For our purposes, periodicals will be divided into *consumer magazines,* the ones that most of us read; and *business, trade,* and *professional publications.* The latter makes up more than 90 percent of the total and may range in circulation from a few thousand to hundreds of thousands, but seldom reach the multimillion circulation figures attained by many popular consumer magazines.

CONSUMER MAGAZINES

There are some 4,000 consumer magazines being distributed in the United States today through some 155,000 retail outlets, including food stores, chain drugstores, convenience stores, discount department stores, newsstands, and bookstores. This is the figure supplied by the CPDA, the Council for Periodical Distributors Association. The Magazine Store in New York's Times Square, selling only magazines and a few stationery items, carries more than 1,000 publications. Part of the problem in determining the exact number of consumer magazines is that there are usually up to six hundred new ones started each year, of which perhaps 10 percent will survive to a second year.

The consumer magazines range all the way from the familiar covers we see at supermarket checkout counters to such special-interest publications as *American Film, Stereo Review,* and *Golf Digest,* from *Sew Magazine* and *Modern Bride* to *Woodenboat* and *Soldier of Fortune,* a magazine for mercenaries. Such publications are considered "special interest" because they are intended for a consumer audience with a clearly defined interest. A professional photographer, for example, may have an interest in tennis and would be naturally drawn to a magazine such as *World Tennis,* as well as periodicals such as *Studio Photography* or *Technical Photography,* which are essential in his or her work.

Among consumer magazines, according to *Standard Rate and Data Service* listings, the largest number of titles are found in categories such as sports. Then there are titles of general interest to women; "shelter magazines" covering the broad field of homes, gardens, and interior decorating; magazines dedicated to travel; and magazines concerned only with automobiles.

BUSINESS, TRADE, AND PROFESSIONAL MAGAZINES

In the immense field of business, trade, and professional magazines there are giant publishing houses, such as Cahners (Reed), McGraw-Hill, and Penton IPC, as well as countless highly successful smaller publishing companies that often dominate the fields they serve. In addition, there are more than 17,000 trade and professional associations, such as the American Bar Association, the National Safety Council, and American Hotel & Motel Associates, that publish magazines to serve their membership.

There is a substantial market out there for talented and motivated young people, and a great many new jobs open up every year. Remember that for every magazine going out of business even more enter the market, sometimes more than one a day.

As with many consumer periodicals, business, trade, and professional magazines are directed to specific interests. Thousands of them are edited for our various industries: law, accounting, plumbing, retailing, and engineering, to name a few. In the medical field alone, there are at least 780 magazines. The health care field has grown significantly in recent years, enough to warrant a separate volume in the *Standard Rate and Data Service* directory of business and trade publications.

No matter what sport you may play or follow as a spectator, it will have its own magazine. If you drive a taxi, you have a choice of several work-related publications. If you are in sales and marketing—well, you'll never be able to catch up with the available magazine reading in your field. Even the magazine business has its own trade journal, *Folio,* which is read cover to cover by the real movers and shakers in the magazine business—as well as those on the way up.

In short, the magazine business is a big, wide, and wonderful world, so enormous that it seems unmanageable, and yet so specific in its editorial direction, so accurately targeted in its circulation, that it zeroes in on an incredible variety of special interests. Consequently, if you go to work in magazine publishing, you might find yourself working for a newsmagazine like *Time* or *Newsweek,* a large-circulation periodical with a general audience like *Reader's Digest* or *People,* or a business, industrial, or trade magazine such as *Brewer's Digest* or *Boxboard Containers.* There is, literally, no end to the opportunities available. You might apply one of your own special interests such as your hobby or avocation into a career in magazine work in that field. Don't make the mistake of assuming that the best jobs are only with the large, well-known consumer magazines. You are likely to get more diversified experience and faster recognition of your efforts working for a smaller magazine.

If you have thoughts of starting your own magazine, be prepared to have enough money on hand to last for two to three years before you become profitable, which can mean an initial investment of hundreds of thousands of dollars. Yet it has been done for less. It is sometimes possible to persuade a printer to finance publication in return for a share of the ownership.

CHAPTER 10

THE SCOPE OF MODERN MAGAZINES

New magazines have a way of responding to the trends and new interests of the public. More recently, magazines have reflected an increasing concern by Americans with health and fitness and what marketers have labeled as a concentration on personal concerns. We now have such publications as *Self, Runner's World, American Health,* and Rodale Press's *Prevention* magazine. Current interests have resulted in a burgeoning group of magazines devoted to women in business: *Working Woman, Working Mother, Savvy Mother,* and *Entrepreneurial Woman,* among others. Nor should we forget the computer magazines, which enjoyed a spectacular boom in the early 1980s that shows no sign of slowing down.

Another phenomenon of our times that was touched on earlier is the city magazine. The numbers increase regularly and represent virtually all the major metropolitan areas. The success of city magazines has boosted the growth of regional and state magazines, such as *Connecticut* and *Texas Monthly,* and of magazines serving high-income resort areas such as *Palm Springs Life.* Far from being merely where-to-go-and-what-to-do periodicals, many of the city magazines now do excellent investigative reporting, in addition to covering life in their communities.

Nothing in the past approached magazines like *Smithsonian, Audubon,* and *National Geographic* as dispensers of cultural information, particularly with the advantage of contemporary craftsmanship in photography and color printing. Graphically, it might be added, there is no comparison between magazines of the present and the past, with no more than two or three exceptions like the *Vanity Fair* and *Vogue* issues of the twenties, with their striking covers and art work. Typography, design, and art work are at a peak today.

We live now in the Age of Information, and certainly magazines are prime carriers. No other country in the world can equal the United States for sheer numbers and variety of magazine publication. Where else, for instance, could there be magazines on skiing and snowmobiling; those devoted to brides and astronomers; magazines on romance—even magazines providing information about UFOs.

Newsletters should not be neglected in this survey. Technically they may not be magazines by some definitions, but they do provide information to their readers. There are more than four thousand of them, covering a wide variety of subjects, ranging all the way from hastily done, amateurish productions distributed free to highly professional, well-written and well-produced publications for professionals willing to pay hundreds, sometimes thousands, of dollars for an annual subscription. Those published weekly have the advantage of timeliness, directing information to readers quickly in fields that change rapidly.

JOB OPPORTUNITIES ON CONSUMER MAGAZINES

What is it like to work for a consumer magazine, and why should any distinction be made between consumer magazines and business, trade, and industrial publications? This is a natural question, but because of the complexity of the magazine business, there is no simple answer.

The profiles of consumer magazines vary widely, depending on a number of characteristics such as circulation, audience, and editorial content. Circulation might range from a few hundred copies to *TV Guide*'s more than fifteen million. In the editorial area there are, for one example, politically oriented magazines devoted to a special cause such as William Buckley's *National Review* or quite narrowly focused special-interest magazines like *Lottery Player Magazine* and *Soap Opera Digest.* There are large general-interest magazines such as *People* and *US* and everything in between. There are local magazines such as *Los Angeles* and *South Florida.*

Whether you consider consumer or business magazines, many of the job functions are essentially the same, though the work itself can be quite different.

Organization

There are many different structures in organization, depending on the size of the publication. On small publications, a single person may perform the same functions that would require half-a-dozen or more people to carry out on a large magazine. This can add considerably to the diversification of the work and the experience you will receive.

In a large publishing house, magazines may be organized by title, with each publication serving as a profit center and having its own staff working closely together—an attempt, in effect, to retain the personal aspect of publishing. Or, the multimagazine company may be organized by function, centralizing as many different activities as possible, such as circulation, production, and finance, to serve all the magazines within the company rather than each magazine having a separate staff for these jobs.

To carry out all these duties, the magazine facility may be situated in a small suite of offices, or it may require several floors in a large building, or, in some cases, it may occupy its own building. The actual printing and binding of the magazine is likely to be done outside the company's office, generally by an independent supplier. Keep in mind that a publisher publishes and a printer prints. The publisher creates and the printer manufactures. They are two separate businesses.

Editorial Functions

What is a day on a magazine like? On smaller magazines, where a few people do the work, the hours may be flexible and can easily include evening and weekend work to meet deadlines. People at the top on all magazine staffs habitually work very long hours and often work at least part of Saturday and Sunday.

The frequency of the magazine's issues makes some difference, although the pressure of deadlines is likely to seem as great on a monthly as on a weekly. The staffs of consumer monthlies customarily work three months ahead of cover date—that is, at any one time there are three issues in the works: one about to be published, one being prepared for publication, and one in the planning stage. Editors must think not only in terms of the three, but must be working on even longer-range plans. Special Christmas editions, for example, are usually in the planning stage by July. Weeklies operate more like newspapers, with each department doing its own work, which fits into a system that continues from week to week.

Although magazine business operations are fundamentally alike no matter what their size, the character of editorial department work is much more affected by the size of the magazine. Broadly speaking, editorial department people are engaged in doing three things: planning, processing materials, and manufacturing.

Planning is done mostly at the top, by the editor, the chief associate or senior editors, and often by the publisher as well. Processing is performed by those farther down the ladder: assistant editors, associate editors, and editorial assistants. They are the people who edit the copy, read the proofs, copyedit, sometimes rewrite, occasionally deal with authors and agents (ordinarily done on the highest editorial level), and, in short, prepare an issue for publication. Picture selection and preparation are needed, and similar planning is simultaneously taking place in the advertising department. Ad pages are assembled by the art department, and the final act of manufacturing is done by the printer under the watchful eyes of the editorial and production departments.

In general, most consumer magazines (and many of the specialized ones) begin the process of getting out an issue by drawing from the pool of available material. It's a large pool, filled with manuscripts, a few that come in unsolicited, but primarily manuscripts that have been written by writers who have been engaged by the magazine, based on ideas developed by editors.

Common practice (and as always, there are numerous variations) is to decide on the contents of a given issue through the give-and-take of an editorial conference. In making their selections, the editors must think about timeliness, about what their competitors are currently doing, and then try to strike a balance in the contents so that one subject or one kind of article does not heavily outweigh the others.

Production Functions

Changes are often made right up to the last minute. Something in the news may diminish or destroy the timeliness of an article, or perhaps a manuscript will arrive in the office unexpectedly that demands immediate publication, or on occasion an editor may simply have a change of mind and abandon one piece for another.

Then begins the production process, going on simultaneously in the various departments of the magazine. The art department is selecting the photographs, illustrations, or whatever else is needed graphically. The advertising department is selling as many ads as possible for the issue and making sure the ad copy arrives on schedule. When it is done, or at the proper moment, the layout people will be able to put pages together to format the complete magazine. Meanwhile, the front cover has been prepared, often with the help of the circulation and promotion people.

Cover selection is an important factor for a consumer magazine that depends on its sale on the newsstands, where it competes with many other titles. Understandably, then, cover selection is even more important today, when there are so many more magazines competing for display space at retail outlets. Remember, the magazine is a consumer product and needs packaging that will arouse interest and motivate the consumer to buy.

Newsmagazines

One group of consumer magazines that share many of the characteristics of business publications, but on a much larger scale, are the newsmagazines such as *Time, Newsweek,* and *U.S. News and World Report.* Their timeliness also means that the staff must constantly be prepared for last-minute changes.

The nature of a newsweekly calls for reports and comments on the current local, national, and international scenes for readers who also probably read one or two newspapers, five or six special-interest consumer magazines, and listen to news on the car radio and watch news shows on television. They also are probably up on the newest books and are interested in movies, theater, and the arts. Therefore, they demand something special in a newsmagazine's coverage. That means the magazine needs to have outstanding correspondents in major cities and foreign capitals. The magazine needs good writers, a comprehensive library for research, a picture collection, researchers to check facts, and abundant freelance as well as staff photographers. Covers must be timely and often acted upon at the last minute.

New technology has made a world of difference in the way writers and editors work today. Gone are the old manual typewriters, and even the electric typewriters; gone the linotype machines of old. Computer typesetting and satellite transmission of printed material have been a boon to newsmagazines. Writers, editors, and copy editors work on the story, editing as they go, writing and rewriting on their computer terminals. When the story is completed, it is electronically set in type. Proofs of the story are then supplied to makeup editors, who supply photostats or copies of the illustrations required and then submit a dummy of the issue, page by page, to the editor-in-chief for a final reading and approval.

Then, it is time to send the whole business to the printing plant, these days often done electronically. But suppose there's a last-minute headline story. If it's a particularly big event—a major disaster or the death of a world leader—the whole issue can be reworked, even at the last minute, to accommodate a new cover story. Sometimes, of course, it's too late. One big biweekly was stuck with a flossy fashion article in the issue that appeared on the stands the week after President John F. Kennedy was assassinated. In some instances, the magazine will be prepared to shift emphasis ahead of time. A postelection issue, for example, will probably have two covers prepared—one for each candidate.

WORKING FOR BUSINESS, TECHNICAL, AND TRADE MAGAZINES

Numerically, by far the largest segment of the magazine business is the business press, an immensely varied kind of publishing intended to serve those engaged in particular businesses. Nearly every kind of occupation has at least one magazine, and these magazines proliferate as technology introduces new businesses and creates new magazines.

Collectively, these business magazines have been known as "the trade press," an easy but inaccurate term to be applied to so many different kinds of periodicals. For years, too, they were known as the poorhouse of the magazine industry, where salaries were low and the work hard. Since many talented young people preferred to work on the more glamorous consumer magazines, the old trade press got what remained of the talent pool. The editors in those days were likely to be former salespeople in the industry that the magazine served, and having risen from the sales ranks, saw the periodical as a sales tool rather than an editorial product. Consequently, the business press had a deserved reputation for being dull.

Those days are gone. Salaries in the business press are now much higher, if not always comparable with the best consumer magazines. Editors are usually professional magazine people who look at their product in much the same way consumer magazine editors regard their publications. Business magazines may still seem dull to people not involved in a particular business, but for the most part they are well written and edited. Their graphic design is frequently outstanding, to be compared with the best consumer magazines; and taken together, they constitute the largest reservoir of information in the world.

The Broad Scope of the Business Press

Some attempt has been made to define the field by the American Business Press, the industry trade association to which most of the larger publishing houses belong. The ABP, as it is familiarly known, defines its members as "specialized business publications serving specific industrial business, service, or professional business audiences, not including general businesses or business news magazines." This definition thus excludes such magazines as *Business Week, Forbes,* and *Fortune,* which are categorized as general consumer publications. So large is the business press, however, that the ABP's membership accounts for little more than a fourth of all business publications. The ABP's records indicate that the number of business publications has grown steadily during the past twenty years, with as many startups each year as closures. Annually, these magazines rack up advertising revenues in the billions.

Business publications fall into various categories, each serving a specialized interest, as follows:

- *Technical and industrial* publications edited for engineering and scientific people.
- *Professional* publications for doctors, lawyers, accountants, educators, and others.
- *Merchandising and trade* publications for retail trades as well as industries such as hotels, banks, trucking firms, and even undertakers.

In each of these categories you find publications to serve different needs. Therefore, for a field like advertising, the publications include those that serve the creative side of the business, others that serve media and research, and general news publications such as *Advertising Age,* which is published weekly and is read in all advertising disciplines.

The extent of business, technical, and trade publishing might be described as one of the world's better-kept secrets. Because these publications are not distributed on newsstands or by open subscription, most people are not aware of their existence until they join the work force, at which time they become acquainted with the publications serving the field they have entered. The business press is international. Few nations, except for the developing countries, are without a business press of some kind.

Just as consumer magazines educate, entertain, and inform the general public and aim to appeal to readers on the basis of demographic characteristics such as age, sex, and intellectual and income levels, so business publications appeal to readers on the basis of their job responsibilities. People who go to work for a business publication, or who encounter them for the first time, are often amazed by the size of many of these magazines.

Organization

Working on the editorial staff of a business magazine that concentrates on the news of an industry is not unlike working for a newspaper. A business publication that stresses feature articles on the industry it serves will generally have an editorial staff similar to many consumer magazines. There is, understandably, a great deal of variation in editorial purpose among these many thousands of publications. With regard to editorial staff, business publications can be staff-written or largely dependent on freelance writers, or a combination of both. This varies with the industry and the type of publication, although it can be generally said that business magazines rely less heavily on outside writers than do consumer magazines.

On a business paper, the editor looks at the industry he or she serves much as the editor of a newspaper looks at the community in which the paper is published. The news is about current events, people, and trends, and along with this is supplied a quantity of information including new product data, coverage of industry trade shows, and much more. The newspaper and the consumer magazine also entertain to some degree; the business magazine does not.

Once the information has been gathered, copy is written, then edited by associate or assistant editors, then copyedited either by a department doing only that or more often by a junior staff member. Photography and artwork are prepared in the same way as on consumer magazines, and the production and advertising departments do the same kind of work, right through the printing process.

Circulation

Circulation, however, is an entirely different matter for a business or trade magazine. Consumer magazines go to some 175,000 or more retail outlets in the United States and Canada, but business, technical, and trade magazines are generally distributed only by mail to their readers. This circulation is obtained in a variety of ways.

Regular paid circulation is made up of paid reader subscriptions to the magazine, which are the same as paid subscriptions to consumer magazines. The most popular form of circulation for business publications, however, is "controlled" circulation, which means that the magazine is sent free of charge to its readers. This form of circulation for business, technical, and trade publications enables the publisher to reach every important buying influence in a market, which is very appealing to advertisers who wish to reach this audience.

Similarly, association-owned magazines are distributed to the members of the organization and may be distributed at no charge, or a subscription price may be built into the annual membership dues.

There are some magazines in which both paid and controlled circulation are mixed; subscriptions are solicited, but the magazine is still distributed free to its target audience. The largest-circulation magazines in America today are published by the American Association of Retired Persons (AARP) and sent free to all dues-paying members. Though generally considered a consumer magazine because of its general editorial content, *Modern Maturity*'s circulation is entirely controlled by the membership roster, as is the *NRTA/AARP Bulletin*. Their circulation is likely to continue to grow, considering demographic predictions about the "graying of America." By the year 2020, one out of every five Americans will be over the age of sixty-five.

In-House Publications

Although they belong in this category, house organs and plant newspapers are in a class by themselves. Collectively they are known as in-house publications and house organs, with these terms often used in an ambiguous way. There are more than ten thousand of them, and they range in size from modest eight-page magazines, almost newsletters (and sometimes they are), in small organizations to prosperous-looking publications put out by the largest corporations.

House organs serve several different purposes. They are often meant to be a communications bridge between management and workers, which means they are customarily scorned by union leaders, who have generated their own newspapers and magazines. The labor press, however, has attracted only small audiences, while company house organs have flourished. They express management viewpoints, which are probably largely ignored, but they are also filled with personal news about events in the lives of employees—marriages, births, deaths—the stuff of small-town weeklies. Whether they also inspire company loyalty and improve morale, as management hopes, is open to question.

Working for house organs is not the same as working for the business magazines described earlier. The overall structure and organization are the same, and the reporting and editing are not much different. But the focus is limited. Rather than a whole industry or occupation, one unit of an industry is being covered, and in a more personal way for an audience physically visible every day, in the case of internal house organs. These publications are more likely to bear the stamp of the editor-in-chief, who is sometimes an officer of the company. That usually occurs when the magazine is part of the public relations or industrial relations department of a company and is seen as a management tool.

To work for such a publication, then, means that the writers and editors must faithfully reflect company viewpoints and attitudes; must be content to see their work constantly reviewed for any deviation from policy, intended or not; and must understand that they are simply the transmitters of whatever information the company wants dispensed.

Once that is understood and accepted, employees of these publications often find their work enjoyable, although salary scales are not usually as high as those of the workers the magazine covers.

CHAPTER 11

PREPARING FOR A MAGAZINE CAREER

BASIC SKILLS AND EDUCATION

What about education? How does one go about preparing for a magazine publishing career?

In one sense, preparing to go into the magazine business is similar to the preparation required for book publishing. Everything you can learn will be useful. Since magazines, like books, deal in ideas, it helps to have the broadest possible background of knowledge. Well-educated people have a decided edge.

But there is a difference. Book publishing moves at a slower pace, and deadlines are more rigidly enforced in magazine publishing. There's little time to gaze at the scenery out of your office window. In book publishing, the edited, published product is what contributes to the profit of the company. In magazine publishing, the profit comes from advertising and circulation. Therefore, in magazine publishing, the sales and marketing functions carry more influence. On the editorial side, knowledge of a specific subject can help land a job with a magazine devoted to that subject.

Here we come to the ancient argument that journalism school graduates have had to contend with for so many decades: on-the-job training versus college preparation. Of course anyone with ability can learn on the job and perhaps, in the end, can do just as well as someone with a degree from a first-class university. The advantage of the latter preparation, although not invariably true, is that a graduate who has learned basic skills and has some background in the field comes to the *first* job with something to offer—maybe not a great deal by some measurements, but at least practical skills that can be employed at once. Thus, special education helps not only in getting the job, but career development time is saved if the new employee has some expertise along with the basic skills. On-the-job training time can be skipped or shortened, and the rise up the ladder consequently accelerated, all else being equal.

Students enrolled in journalism schools and departments who have decided on magazine work as a career will find it helpful to take such courses as photography, editorial or interpretive writing or interpretative journalism (these courses have various names), newswriting, editing, and communications law. Outside electives might include courses in history, political science, and economics. People with an interest in prospective management or sales positions should also take marketing and advertising courses.

NONCOLLEGE COURSES

Even if you're not going to college, this road is still open to you. Production skills can be learned in adult education classes at relatively small costs. Printing Industries of America, Inc. (PIA) sponsors courses on printing and production in large cities throughout America. You can find out more about their locations and schedules by writing: Printing Industries of America, Inc., 100 Daingerfield Road, Alexandria, Virginia 22314. Specialized knowledge is always available in books to supplement what you have learned elsewhere about your area of interest, either from practical experience or self-study. By looking in the library at standard directories of magazines, you will be able to identify the periodicals toward which you want to aim. The rest is up to you.

GETTING STARTED

There are so many ways to get started in magazine work that aspirants understandably often are confused. From the outside looking in, the magazine world looks so immense that career seekers scarcely know where or how to begin. Obviously, a great deal depends on the individual, but there are some general guideposts.

Getting the first job, of course, is the first goal. You will hear it said in many quarters that jobs are hard to get, and that is true. Jobs are always hard to get in any part of the communications business because supply always exceeds demand; this is especially true for entry-level jobs. The magazine industry, by virtue of its sheer size and the number and variety of publications being issued, offers much better opportunities simply because there are so many more jobs to be filled. So people who are looking for work should remind themselves that jobs do exist and that they are filled every day.

Another general observation: It's always much easier to get another job if you already have one, so don't refuse a position because it's not the one you want or the magazine you want to work for. The most important task is getting the first job, whatever or wherever it may be. You can learn from it, no matter what it is, and after a period of time you'll find it much easier to find another job because you will have experience to offer and no doubt more skills and knowledge at your command.

Let's go back to the vital business of getting the first job. At the very least, make an initial choice between consumer magazines or business magazines. That will affect your plan of action immediately. If it's to be consumer magazines, especially the big, important ones we see every day on the newsstands, the strategy is different than it is for looking for work on trade magazines in a particular field.

WHERE THE JOBS ARE

If you choose the major consumer magazines, you most likely will have to go to New York City because, with a few exceptions, that's where the offices of nearly all these magazines are. The magazine business is centered there, although periodicals, especially many of the business and professional publications, are also published in every major city and many smaller communities. Washington, DC, is the second-largest center because of the United States government's vast publication program and the fact that the Washington area is headquarters for many associations. Then there are such important magazines as the *Atlantic Monthly* in Boston; *Playboy* in Chicago; *TV Guide* in Radnor, Pennsylvania; the *Reader's Digest* in Pleasantville, New York; and the fast-growing city magazines, which can be found in most cities of a million or more in population.

Getting a job on a major consumer magazine, the goal of many journalism graduates, is the hardest task of all, but it can be done. You need to make another decision, however, before you start. What part of the consumer field interests you most? Is it the women's magazines, the newsmagazines, the men's magazines, the literary magazines? The choice is even wider, of course, and each type presents its particular problems. A good way to begin is to examine carefully every magazine in the area you've chosen. Read the mastheads and familiarize yourself with the names of the staff. Observe how the magazine is put together, what departments it has, what kinds of articles it runs. Your prospective employer will want to know, among other things, why you want to work for that particular periodical.

It isn't always necessary to start at the bottom. If you can bring particular knowledge or expertise to a magazine, and have at least some experience, it's possible to begin higher up. A rapid rise in the ranks is also possible even if the first job is entry level, particularly on small magazines and on those where there is a fairly rapid personnel turnover.

JOB-SEEKING METHODS

Unsolicited Applications

As with books and newspapers, the standard methods of job hunting should not be neglected in looking for jobs on the other magazines. With newsmagazines, the best approach (lacking personal influence) is to register with the personnel department and keep calling back from time to time. On other consumer publications, registering with the personnel department is always advisable in any case.

Classified Ads

Don't forget the classified ads. Look under "Publishing," "Editorial," "Circulation," and "Advertising Sales" in the major newspapers. You might also consult the classified ads in the various trade publications themselves.

In the business press field, the American Business Press in New York City has a job placement service in a monthly newsletter called *Employment Roundup*. The *Roundup* carries both help-wanted ads placed by ABP member publishers and position-wanted ads placed by anyone interested in a job in the business publishing field. Once job seekers have completed the ABP placement service application form, the placement service director can include their own ads, stating their objectives and qualifications, and job seekers can be assured that members of the ABP will receive this information.

An online search using keywords such as "jobs" and "magazines" will bring you to a wealth of contacts. Most print magazines have websites, and of course, all electronic ones do. Some professional associations also maintain job banks. (See Appendix A.)

Employment Agencies

Some employment agencies specialize in magazine and publishing jobs, and you can find them by looking in the trade journals. In visiting the agencies, be prepared to find yourself in the hands of hard-boiled, realistic people who will be likely to treat you as though you were a piece of merchandise. They know where at least some of the jobs are, and they will make the contact for an interview, also exacting a fee from you if you get the job, unless the employer pays it. Agencies handle jobs for both consumer and trade magazines, ranging all the way from entry level to top level. It pays to register with two or three of them.

The Resume

The first thing an agency will request (and most employers demand the same thing) is a resume. They're important, and you need to have the best one you can devise. If you don't know anything about putting one together, try one of the following books, all published by VGM Career Books: *Resumes for the First-Time Job Hunter, Resumes for College Students and Recent Graduates,* and *Resumes for Communications Careers.* Any of these are available at your favorite bookstore.

Include in your resume any kind of work you've ever done—extracurricular work on high school and college publications, jobs with organizations, and even summer jobs, no matter how menial they may have been or how unrelated to magazine work. They will add up to more than you may have thought at the start.

At the top of your resume should be a paragraph titled "Job Objective." The two things a prospective employer wants to know are what you know and have done, and what you want to do. If one asks, "What kind of job do you want with us?" *be specific.* Say, "I want a job as editorial assistant [or any other job you know is entry level] so I can learn the business." You should know titles and duties of entry-level jobs.

The Interview

Before you can get your foot on the first rung of the ladder, you have to get it in the door. Obtaining an interview isn't always a matter of simply sending in your resume and waiting for the telephone to ring. The following method for job seeking can be used by graduates looking for jobs in the magazine industry: Make a list of all the periodicals in the particular area where you want to work and, using the standard guides for this purpose, write down the names of the editors and executives. Write letters to all of them, telling them briefly about yourself, enclosing a resume, and asking for an interview. Experience shows that out of a hundred names, you should get about a dozen responses, and of these, five or six are likely to result in interviews.

Now, let's suppose that you have obtained an interview with an editor or possibly a personnel director, someone in a position to hire you. The interview is a critical step. It's important to dress for the occasion. This does not mean dressing in an excessively conservative fashion, since people in the communications business are likely to wear work clothes today that would have been considered sloppy a few years ago. But even though you may wind up wearing jeans on the job (not every day nor in all jobs), don't wear them to the interview. For both men and women, the image to be presented is one of simple neatness. Times may have changed, but they haven't changed that much. Neatness still counts, and flamboyance is usually viewed askance.

This advice applies, in a sense, to the spoken impression as well as to the visual one. Don't try to overwhelm the interviewer with your personality. Be straightforward, simple, frank, and above all, honest. *Here's How: Have a Winning Job In-*

terview and *How to Get Hired Today!,* both published by VGM Career Books, are good sources to help you maximize your potential when you interview.

STARTING YOUR OWN MAGAZINE

In every university or workshop magazine class, there are always students who say, "I don't want to work for anybody. I want to start my own magazine." There was a time when professors gently discouraged anyone with such ideas, unless the ambitious one had a rich uncle. But today, even with the staggering costs brought on by inflation, it is actually easier to start a magazine than it was in the past. This is largely due to the lower costs involved in new production and printing technology.

Not many students with this ambition succeed in realizing their ideas for a new magazine, but some do, and of the more than one hundred new magazines begun every year, there are always some started by bold young entrepreneurs with little more than courage, a small amount of capital, and high confidence in their ideas. For those people, any discussion of getting started should offer a few guidelines.

Money is the essential ingredient in starting a new magazine, but it is not the only necessary one. Experience is another essential. Magazines have been started by people without any magazine experience, and some have succeeded, but the odds are high that they will not. Even those who have come into the business with successful records in other fields can bankrupt themselves quickly in periodical publishing.

Another important predetermining factor is whether it will be possible to get enough advertising, the lifeblood of nearly every magazine. Getting advertising for a new magazine is one of the most difficult problems a would-be entrepreneur has to solve. Most advertisers and their agencies want to wait and see whether the magazine will survive, but by that time it will be too late for the publisher.

Make Your Beginning

Clearly, there are many ways to get started in the business of magazines, from the lowly entry-level job to the exciting prospect of starting a magazine of your own. But if you are in love with the magazines, you'll enter by whichever door opens to you.

The important thing is to get started, work at the best job you can get, learn as much as you can, and learn well. Then, make your plans and move upward.

CHAPTER 12

JOBS IN MAGAZINE PUBLISHING

Success in the competitive and diversified magazine business requires highly specialized skills and a number of activities:

First, editorial matter must be created to compete favorably and appeal to a defined audience. This material must reflect the basic reason for the magazine's existence in its writing, graphics, and photography.

Second, the magazine must be marketed to its readers, a function that calls into play all the modern techniques to induce the public to buy it: print advertising, publicity, sales promotion, direct response, radio, television, outdoor advertising. No sales technique is ignored by successful magazine publishers. Marketing calls for talented copywriters, designers, direct-marketing experts, and the most ingenious and comprehensive kinds of strategies and tactics.

Third, advertisers must be sold on the publication if it is to be financially profitable. Advertising sales requires persuasion, backed up by an intimate knowledge of the magazine, and targeted market research that delves into the audience demographics—that is, educational level, income, age, home ownership, and buying habits. Advertisers now also want information on what are known as psychographics, the study of human motivation and buying attitudes.

Fourth, the magazine must be printed and distributed. To accomplish this fundamental task, the following skills are required: knowledge of printing techniques; an understanding of paper, price, and quality; distribution channels; and much more.

Finally, a magazine staff needs personnel with the same general skills useful in any business: the management of people, the ability to master large amounts of detail while keeping the basic objectives in clear view, concentration, and the ability to function under pressure. Few of these qualities are innate in any human being; most can be learned through experience.

THE PUBLISHER

The "publisher at the top" may or may not have genius but is invariably a "jack of all trades," with a combination of skills that enables him or her to work well with creative people and inspire and direct salespeople. This person also possesses the knowledge of printing production and circulation necessary to ensure a successful business operation. This type of structure is generally found in owner-managed publishing companies.

Where responsibility is departmentalized, the publisher's job is more clearly limited. In general, the publisher is the person who is in charge of advertising sales and advertising sales promotion. This structure is generally found in larger publishing firms, where functions such as production, circulation, finance, and administration are assumed by corporate departments that serve all publishing units in the company. In such instances, the publisher may also be involved with budgeting, profit-and-loss projections, and other management functions. The publisher works closely with corporate-level people.

THE EDITORIAL DEPARTMENT

Editor-in-Chief

Directly under the publisher on the editorial side may be an executive editor, sometimes called editor-in-chief, who is directly responsible for the magazine's day-to-day editorial operation. This person is charged with implementing the editorial policy of the magazine, except for policy questions that might require an answer from a higher authority—spending an unusual amount of money, for example, or changing the editorial format or emphasis or direction of the magazine.

The editor is, in fact, the second most important person on the magazine's staff, second only to the publisher. The editor-in-chief is the person whose feelings and tastes and ideas shape the magazine's personality until it becomes a living thing. Great magazines nearly always bear the stamp of great editors.

The Managing Editor

The next most important job in the editorial hierarchy is that of managing editor, an entirely different kind of position with its own special responsibilities. A managing editor is sometimes called the "traffic cop" of a magazine because he or she must direct the flow of material as it goes through the department. The managing editor lives by schedules—the issue schedule, the printer's schedule, and others that chart the course of everything that goes into the magazine. Putting it another way, the managing editor is the chief operating officer of the editorial department, while the editor-in-chief is the chief executive officer.

Managing editors usually attend editorial conferences as plans for an issue are developed. It is the managing editor who sees that these plans are carried out. Managing editors route the copy from the other editorial staff members, send it to the printer, get the proofs and see that they are read, supervise the schedule that leads to production of the cover, perform the same functions for advertising copy, and coordinate all these schedules so that they come together on time at the printing plant.

Managing editors must have the ability to organize, to enlist the cooperation of the entire staff, to make decisions, and, above all, to take responsibility for getting the magazine out on schedule. Missing deadlines can create havoc with a magazine's budget. Most managing editors, although not all of them, have a university degree in journalism and perhaps ten years of experience in newspapers, magazines, or related fields. No matter what the size of the magazine, managing editors have an exacting job, and no one without a superior talent for handling detail, and a liking for it, should aspire to this position. The best managing editors are so valuable that they are paid handsomely on the major magazines, but on smaller periodicals they are inclined to be workhorses, paid on the same scale as the associate editors.

Senior, Associate, and Assistant Editors

Associate or senior editors, and on the next layer below, the assistant editors, have roughly the same kind of job, except that the more important parts of it are entrusted to the higher-ranking people. Everyone, however, is supposed to be thinking of article ideas for the magazine. Some material comes from literary agents, who represent professional magazine writers; more comes from writers who represent themselves; and a tiny fraction may come from the pile of unsolicited manuscripts, but a high percentage of what is finally printed—the ratio varies from magazine to magazine—originates with the editors.

Editors must be people who are fertile with ideas for the magazine, and they must also be able to edit articles, rewrite them if necessary, copyedit them if the magazine does not have a copy editor, and read proof. An editor is responsible, if there is no copy editor, for spotting errors of every kind in a manuscript.

To succeed in this department requires a good educational background (unless you're a self-taught genius), a firm grasp of how to use the English language, a good sense of style, and at least some expertise in whatever field the magazine covers. People with broad general backgrounds can move from one magazine to another without much trouble; others prefer to use their expertise in a given area on one magazine that serves people who share their interests.

Associate or *senior editors* are part writers, part editors. They work extensively with other writers on assigning, editing, or rewriting stories. Or they may write stories under their own bylines. They should be self-starters, capable of pitching into any aspect of the editorial operation, depending on the magazine's needs. It's no easy matter to work as an editor with other writers, and as a writer with other editors, but somehow the associate editor must carry off such a dichotomy.

Assistant editors, or sometimes *editorial assistants,* are on the lowest rung of the departmental ladder. On large magazines, one of the first things they were once called upon to do was to go through the several hundred unsolicited manuscripts flooding in every day in search of new talent or ideas. There is much less of that today because many of the major magazines now do not accept unsolicited manuscripts, simply because the flood became too great and handling it was excessively costly in time and money. People with ideas are asked to send outlines, and if these sound promising, they are invited to submit manuscripts.

Assistant editors have the opportunity to attend story conferences, submit ideas, and work with freelancers. They may also do some writing, as well as helping with general editing.

Contributing Editors

Contributing editors are people whose names are listed on the masthead, but who are usually not on staff. Basically, they're freelance writers with a record of producing ideas and articles prolifically or perhaps contributing a regular column on a specific subject. They are often on a retainer, in return for which they must produce a certain number of pieces or a regular column. The most important characteristics for success in this type of work are self-discipline and the ability to work without prodding or supervision.

Salaries

There is a wide range of pay in editorial work. Tables 1 through 7 give average salary figures for various editorial, management, production, and sales positions.

Table 1. Average Editorial Salaries, 1999

	Business/Trade Magazines	*Consumer Magazines*
Editors-in-Chief/ Editorial Directors	$80,100	$78,100
Editors/Executive Editors	$55,000	$47,000
Managing Editors	$51,000	$56,000
Senior Editors	$42,000	$44,000

Source: *Folio: The Magazine for Management,* "1999 Editorial Salary Survey"

According to the *Folio* survey, female managing editors fared better in 1999 than their male counterparts in pay and were almost on par when it came to increases.

For editorial directors, both sexes were also compensated at the same pace, but at dramatically different levels, amounting to approximately $7,000 less for women. Respondents reported added responsibility without added pay and included a wide range of activities—from new media and conference management, to media relations and, of course, websites. The underestimation of the value of editorial was mentioned frequently as a reason for inadequate pay. An editor from the New York City area is quoted as saying: "We're seen as an expense that does not contribute to sales."

Nevertheless, more than sixty editorial professionals stated they were fairly compensated for their considerable workload, many pointing to nonmonetary benefits.

Tables 2 and 3 give senior editor and editorial director average salaries for 1999.

Table 2.   Senior Editor Average Salaries, 1999

	Average	*Average Business*	*Average Consumer*
BY AGE			
Up to 29	$41,195	$36,690	$ —
30–39	54,671	49,957	61,250
40–49	53,327	—	59,143
50 +	59,072	—	59,805
RESPONSIBLE FOR			
1–2 magazines	53,048	46,334	56,500
More than 2	52,729	46,015	—
BY CIRCULATION			
Up to 19,999	—	—	—
20,000–49,999	39,581	42,245	—
50,000–99,999	46,085	44,924	—
100,000–499,999	51,566	—	51,540
500,000 or more	69,966	68,000	70,091

—Not enough information supplied to report results
Source: *Folio: The Magazine for Management,* "1999 Editorial Salary Survey"

Table 3.   Editorial Director Average Salaries, 1999

	Average	*Average Business*	*Average Consumer*
BY AGE			
Up to 29	$ 36,380	$ —	$ —
30–39	70,373	62,500	76,233
40–49	91,531	83,817	101,143
50 +	80,333	88,313	70,433
RESPONSIBLE FOR			
1–2 magazines	$ 76,206	75,635	76,725
More than 2	82,007	79,604	84,775
BY CIRCULATION			
Up to 19,999	$ 52,493	60,321	—
20,000–49,999	71,915	76,545	—
50,000–99,999	73,410	80,169	60,833
100,000–499,999	94,794	111,746	90,194
500,000 or more	104,000	—	104,000

—Not enough information supplied to report results
Source: *Folio: The Magazine for Management,* "1999 Editorial Salary Survey"

THE ART DIRECTOR

The individual most responsible for the magazine's appearance is the art director. Art directors acquire reputations for the distinctive stamp they put on a magazine's appearance. The best of them—those at the top—are much admired and highly paid, in figures sometimes above $100,000 per year.

A gifted art director can transform a whole magazine. Taking it piece by piece, the art director can present articles and pictures in a way that command attention from the reader. The tools of the trade are type, photographs, and illustrations. With these, the art director does magic.

Art directors, editors, and circulation directors who want more newsstand sales are not always in agreement, particularly on the matter of covers, where the art director is likely to oppose anything he or she regards as an excess of type that may detract from the visual image. But there are really no rights or wrongs to this argument. Innumerable cases could be cited to prove both sides right.

Though the magazine's cover is especially important if the publication is to sell on the newsstand, the design of magazine articles is equally important to involve the reader. The designer must decide to use art, photography, just straight type, or perhaps a combination of two or all three. Publishing consultant John Peter points out: "Magazine design is not a fine art but a fine craft. The art director may be an artist possessing inventive talent and visual skills, but he or she is employed as a communications designer. The art director's aim is to get ideas off the printed page and into the minds of readers as clearly and quickly as possible."

Training and Experience

What does it take to be a successful magazine art director besides natural talent? First of all, experience. Most art directors begin in the production department of a magazine or an advertising agency, and often they have had an art school background or have taken design courses at special schools and universities.

Many of the first-rate graphic design programs are in East Coast schools: the Rhode Island School of Design in Providence, RI; Cooper Union, the School of Visual Arts, and Parsons School of Design in New York City; Pratt Institute in Brooklyn; and the Philadelphia College of Art and the Moore College of Art, both in Philadelphia. One of the best on the West Coast is the Art Center College of Design in Pasadena, California.

Positions and Salaries

Entry-level positions in the art department vary from one magazine to the next, but the titles include *art assistant, designer,* or *assistant to the art director.* The responsibilities in these positions vary from preparing the mechanicals—the actual camera-ready artwork from designs prepared by the art director or graphic designers—to designing page layouts and selecting and editing photographs. Salaries vary as well, depending on the level of responsibility, the size of the magazine, and the geographic location. As with most jobs in the publishing industry, Northeast firms generally pay the highest salaries.

The latest *Folio* salary survey shows an alarming phenomenon for art directors. Salaries are decreasing by age and by the number of titles the employee is responsible for. (This circumstance is reversed for production directors. See Table 5.)

Table 4.   Art Director Average Salaries, 1999

BY AGE	SALARY
30–39	$47,399
50 +	$39,271
RESPONSIBLE FOR	
1 magazine	$52,135
More than 1	$42,077

Source: *Folio: The Magazine for Management,* "1999 Art Director Salary Survey"

THE PRODUCTION DEPARTMENT

The chain of command will vary from one publication to another. At *Family Circle*, the production department calls the shots, and the art director is responsible to production. At *People*, on the other hand, the art director runs the show, and the production staff reports to design.

The extreme importance of the production department and the people who work in it may best be appreciated by examining a magazine's annual budget. Anywhere from 40 percent to 50 percent of its expenses are for production. It is, therefore, crucial that the publisher have an experienced and able production staff, people who can save money on production wherever possible, without compromising quality. Any substantial saving on paper, for example, which can be achieved by a production manager finding a new source, can save pennies per copy and add thousands of dollars in profits.

Production Staff

While the production manager is doing the overall planning and dealing with suppliers, the assistant production manager and the production staff will be checking art boards and seeing that the copy flow, to the printer and back, is on schedule and that quality is upheld at all stages.

Also working in the production department may be an advertising coordinator, who is responsible for working with the advertising sales department, getting ads on time from the client or the agency, checking them for size, color, and content. The entry-level jobs in production have low starting salaries, but there are plenty of opportunities to learn, to take on additional responsibilities, and to earn both additional salary and promotions.

Salaries

On large magazines, there may be two individuals holding managerial responsibility: the production director, who could also be called the vice president for production, and the production manager. The production director would be responsible for negotiating printing contracts, establishing production schedules, and overseeing the production manager in areas of technology and quality control. The production manager is then responsible for the day-to-day operation of the production department.

Salaries for these top positions vary according to the level of responsibility, the size of the magazine, and the geographic location. Consumer magazines pay higher salaries for production than do business magazines—according to the

1999, *Folio* salary survey, about $10,000 more—and the Northeast remains the highest-paying region.

Beginning salaries will vary widely, depending largely on previous experience with computers and design. The entry-level range in production is similar to that in the art department. Those with significant experience on computers may command higher starting salaries.

Table 5.   Production Director Average Salaries, 1999

Consumer Magazines	$66,300
Business/Trade Magazines	$54,900

Source: *Folio: The Magazine for Management,* "1999 Production Director Salary Survey"

Although the dollar amounts differ, production directors and managers on both consumer and business titles realize a consistent increase in pay as they age, as the number of titles they are responsible for increases, and as the circulation of their titles goes up. This is a direct reverse from salaries reported for art directors. (See Table 4.)

Concerns expressed from respondents in this survey follow a familiar pattern from past surveys: too much work unrelated to core duties (such as employee training or selling foreign rights) and no compensation for doing it. One production director states: "Production people are the only true generalists in publishing. We must know the basics of every skill…to get publications out [on time]. And then we are told to transfer to sales if we want to earn more money!"

Not everyone is unhappy, though the percentage is small. Nearly 25 percent of respondents say they believe they are adequately compensated and express some enthusiasm for the range of tasks they are asked to perform. Another production director says, "I have lots of freedom to travel and learn. And I'm very involved with editorial, graphics—lots of things/areas."

THE CIRCULATION DEPARTMENT

The importance of the circulation department is influenced by whether circulation is derived from paid subscriptions or single-copy sales, or if the magazine is distributed free. When the task of obtaining the needed circulation is difficult, the importance of this department is greater.

For example, the publisher of an airline in-flight magazine need only arrange for distribution to the appropriate airports where systems are in place to put copies in the seat pockets. Once the procedure is established, distribution is routine. An association magazine need not search for readers as the magazine is simply mailed to members. In cases like this, the circulation department is essentially a clerical operation.

The circulation department is more important at a consumer magazine, where there is constant pressure to "deliver the numbers" that are so essential to show growth to advertisers who expect a magazine to go up and up in its circulation. Often this leads to hyped circulation, which is not always in the best interest of the advertisers, as expanded circulation does not ensure good readership. For most consumer magazines, circulation is derived from two sources, subscriptions and "single-copy" sales (what used to be called "newsstand" sales, until the newsstands became less important than other retail outlets). It is the job of the circulation department to meet the circulation goals set by management. This number is called the "rate base" for the magazine, that is, a six-month average sale of copies through all sources of distribution. This rate base is used to determine what the magazine will charge for its advertising space.

To quote William H. Scherman, from his book, *How to Get the Right Job in Publishing*: "The circulation director and staff must master an act akin to balancing on a tightrope. If they sell too many subscriptions, they are costing the publisher money, for the advertiser contracts to pay for only the circulation announced on the rate card and no more. But if they do not sell enough of a given issue, that shortfall will soon be known from a periodic audit. And the magazine's advertising salesmen will hear about it in no uncertain terms from the agencies they call on.... For their clients, the advertisers, will have been shortchanged."

The Circulation Director

Many questions remain to be answered by the circulation director after the circulation goal is attained. What is the ideal price for which the magazine should be sold? By subscription? On the newsstand? And what quantities should be sold through each to achieve the right balance? Copies sold by subscription are likely to bring in less income per copy, but they bring in substantial sums of money *in advance,* and this is not a small factor when the cost of money as reflected in interest rates is considered. Some advertisers, however, prefer a magazine with high single-copy sales: proof that the reader wanted the specific issue or wanted the magazine badly enough to go out and pick it up somewhere—a buyer therefore more likely to be a reader. Subscribers, on the other hand, may get the magazine regularly, but it is more difficult to say whether they read each and every issue.

In addition to planning and maintaining the ideal circulation, the director of this department is responsible for keeping statistical records of sales, scheduling mailings, establishing print quantities, negotiating arrangements with subscription agencies and distributors, preparing circulation statements, and interpreting the circulation statistics for the advertising department. The circulation director of a large magazine oversees all aspects of magazine circulation, but the specific tasks are often directed by the subscription sales manager and the single-copy sales manager.

Salaries

In *Folio's* 1999 survey of salaries among magazine circulation professionals, the figures suggested that the circulation size of the magazine (or sometimes multiple magazines) made a sharp difference in the salary rate for circulation directors.

Table 6.   Circulation Management Average Salaries, 1999

	Average	*Average Business*	*Average Consumer*
BY AGE			
Up to 29	$ 41,922	$36,698	$ —
30–39	72,680	70,736	73,865
40–49	81,310	82,800	79,699
50 +	75,944	67,693	—
RESPONSIBLE FOR			
1–2 magazines	$ 61,325	57,669	63,479
More than 2	78,181	72,098	84,931
BY CIRCULATION			
Less than 50,000	$ 46,601	49,881	—
50,000–999,999	63,024	76,442	—
100,000–499,999	77,987	76,533	79,165
500,000 or more	110,574	—	104,464

—Not enough information supplied to report results
Source: *Folio: The Magazine for Management,* "1999 Circulation Management Salary Survey"

ADVERTISING SALES

An advertising department at a magazine has one primary function and that is to sell as many ads as possible. The staff must persuade advertisers and their agencies that their magazine will deliver the most cost-effective audience of buyers who constitute the kind of market the advertiser wants to reach. It is a highly complicated, sophisticated, extremely competitive business, and it demands motivated, persuasive, persistent, and innovative salespeople.

It becomes the job of the magazine advertising salesperson to first sell magazines against television and newspapers as the media to dominate the budget, and then to sell his or her magazine (against, perhaps, a dozen or more competitors) as the most effective publication to dominate the magazine schedule. To complicate matters further, the decision on what will be bought will probably be made jointly between the client and the ad agency. Therefore, the salesperson must seek out all buying influences and sell them all without offending any. Does it sound tough? Yes, it is, but the fun is in the chase and the rewards are in the victory. It's no wonder that the work pays well for those who succeed.

Ad Sales Director

Given how essential it is to the bottom-line profit of the magazine, the battle for the advertiser's budget is a mighty one, waged on many fronts. In magazine sales, the advertising director is the commanding general, and the salespeople are in the frontline trenches. As in any other army, there is need for backup and, in this case, sales support. Hence, the advertising department has audience research and other sales tools, an ad budget of its own to promote the magazine, direct mail, a travel and entertainment budget, and much more.

In many cases, the head of advertising sales carries the title of publisher, which provides prestige with advertisers and prospects and acknowledges within the publishing company that this individual is the real moneymaker for the firm. The position of publisher usually is filled from editorial or ad sales departments, and the nod usually goes to the ad director, if he or she has produced well and shown good business skills. Even when the head of ad sales is the publisher, he or she will continue to make sales calls and attend sales presentations, especially when the stakes are high or the competition is keen.

The advertising director selects, trains, and organizes the best sales staff possible; establishes a budget in line with the magazine's anticipated advertising revenue; plans strategy and leads the way to bring in the most business; and makes sure that the staff has all of the sales tools and promotional support to fulfill the task. The ad director motivates the sales staff and serves as teacher, coach, and cheerleader.

Ad Sales Staff

How about the magazine's salespeople? On large consumer magazines, they are frequently specialists in one or more product categories, such as automotive, food, drugs, liquor, cosmetics, fashion, tobacco, consumer electronics, or travel. These are all categories wherein the advertisers have huge budgets. As specialists they become immersed in their markets. Many have been active in their fields for a number of years; they know the accounts and understand their marketing objectives. On business, industrial, and trade publications, it is equally important to have knowledgeable salespeople. Often an advertising salesperson on an engineering publication is a graduate engineer or has had a previous sales job in the field. For example, a salesperson for a trade publication directed to doctors may have worked for a pharmaceutical company. However, in many other cases, the advertising salesperson is simply a person with good sales skills who develops the knowledge on the job.

People who sell advertising in magazines are called space salespeople. Up until the sixties, women were rarely seen on an advertising staff; today, perhaps as many as half of the people selling for consumer magazines are women, and they are moving in fast on business, industrial, and trade magazines.

Sales reps must be able to present themselves well and to think well on their feet. For the salesperson, personal sales traits weigh more heavily than formal education. To sell successfully, one has to be comfortable with people. As the magazine's official representative, it is important for the salesperson to make a good personal impression and project a favorable image of the magazine. The good salesperson has to have persistence, because the order isn't likely to come on the first visit. It generally takes months or years before the big contract is signed. Meanwhile, the sales representative must find ways to stay in touch by phone, letters, and visits while remaining equally busy being of service to existing clients and working on other new prospects.

The salesperson must also know the magazine's editorial content well and be prepared to sell its merits if questioned or challenged. One advertising manager has put it this way: "If the client accepts the magazine's editorial content as creditable, he'll realize its advertising has credibility, too."

Salaries and Commission Sales

If you're one of the qualified people, and you like the idea of selling magazine advertising, you will probably earn a very good living while meeting some of the most interesting people you'll find anywhere. The 1999 *Folio* survey of magazine advertising salespeople reported that the overall average among salespeople was $82,709 in total compensation, with an average base salary at $52,500.

Not every salesperson works on staff. Besides the space salespeople in a magazine's advertising department, there are also independent *publisher's representatives,* who handle advertising space sales for several magazines. These "reps,"

Table 7. Advertising Average Salaries, 1999

AD SALES DIRECTOR

	Average	Average Business	Average Consumer
BY AGE			
Up to 29	$ 87,050	$ 84,600	$ —
30–39	129,297	139,144	125,877
40–49	108,427	113,150	—
50 +	106,729	—	—
RESPONSIBLE FOR			
1–2 magazines	123,374	115,310	132,754
More than 2	110,177	127,103	99,558
BY CIRCULATION			
Up to 19,999	89,692	89,692	—
20,000–49,999	126,602	140,750	—
50,000–99,999	105,509	111,496	—
100,000–499,999	128,856	160,500	119,571
500,000 or more	129,907	—	112,000
BY REGION			
Northeast	141,786	163,002	130,818
New York City	158,617	163,002	155,500
South	100,734	107,470	92,133
North Central	100,422	92,573	—
West	113,610	133,198	104,443

AD SALESPERSON

	Average	Average Business	Average Consumer
Base salaries	$52,500	$57,800	$45,900
Bonuses	$30,209	$30,453	$29,912

—Not enough information supplied to report results
Source: *Folio: The Magazine for Management,* "1999 Advertising Salary Survey"

as they are called, generally work on commission only—15, 20, or 25 percent, depending on their experience and reputation, as well as on advertising rates and the degree of difficulty in the selling effort of the publication. A "rep" can be a one- or two-person firm covering a specified limited area such as New England or Florida.

There are many advantages in working for a good rep firm. First of all, you are likely to work on more than one magazine, so you will get more diversified experience. If you are a good salesperson, your efforts will be recognized quickly, as the entire organization from top to bottom is committed to advertising space sales. You avoid being locked into a situation that can limit your advancement, which can happen when you are on the staff of a single magazine. In a rep firm, if you are a good salesperson, there is always more to do and more opportunity to boost your reputation and, as a consequence, your income.

Ad Research

Advertising departments also need researchers and research analysts to provide the statistics so necessary for selling advertising. Of course, the advertising agencies' media departments have their own voluminous research upon which to draw. Much of this material comes from such major research organizations as Simmons, which syndicates its studies to agencies, with the cost of the service contingent on the size of the particular agency's billings. What Simmons sells is statistical information about consumer magazine audiences, done on a scientific sampling basis. These surveys provide data on population cross sections measured geographically, economically, educationally, and also according to reading and viewing habits. The findings are called *demographics.* Readers are also measured psychographically. *Psychographics* is the study of *attitudes* toward products or publications. It's an effort to "get inside the consumer's head." When addressed to a publication, this research method measures how respondents rate themselves on each of twenty clusters of adjectives, such as whether they consider themselves affectionate (which includes "passionate," "loving," and "romantic"), broadminded, creative (encompassing "inventive," "imaginative," and "artistic"), or stubborn. It also measures "buying style," which is the determination of people's reasons for choosing certain brands, and their recognition of advertising for a product or group of products.

Armed with statistical information, advertising salespeople go to work dramatizing these findings and creating ideas to convince a particular advertiser that his or her products will sell best in the market the magazine reaches. That makes space selling a creative challenge because the salesperson is not only creating ideas but competing with many other good salespeople.

AD SALES PROMOTION

There are other jobs available in a magazine's advertising department as well. The department usually requires an ad sales promotion manager, who will be in charge of creating and producing materials for the sales force to use in their sales calls—anything from slide presentations to personal letters, media kits, and films. Perhaps the promotion person will need to set up a booth, handle a trade show, or prepare brochures or mailing pieces. The person in this job must not only have creative ability, preferably in both writing and the graphic arts, but be full of ideas and imagination. In effect, the promotion department serves the publisher in the same way an advertising department functions in a manufacturing business.

PROMOTION, PUBLIC RELATIONS, AND PUBLICITY

No matter how brilliantly the editorial staff creates a magazine, nor how handsomely its art and production departments produce it, in the end the magazine may still not enjoy its full potential unless it is promoted aggressively to potential advertisers, newsstand buyers, subscribers, and to the public in general. It has been said that the perception of a magazine is often more important than the magazine itself. This type of work is accomplished by promotion departments and in ordinary public relations and publicity efforts.

Promotion

Promotion is directed to boost advertising sales, to sell circulation, and to promote readership. The first may well be the most valuable, given the importance of advertising to the survival of most magazines. The task here is to promote the magazine directly to advertisers to persuade them to buy space.

One promotion device is the mailing of complimentary copies of the magazine to a list of current and prospective advertisers, opinion makers, politicians, and anyone else who might conceivably be interested in what the magazine is doing. This serves the double purpose of calling attention to the publication itself, making those who might help its fortunes aware of what is happening, and at the same time stimulating new advertising.

Magazines often have booths at national conventions that are attended by readers or by businesses whose advertising they hope to attract. To increase subscriptions, some magazines use their exhibition booths at conventions to sign up new readers, perhaps offering special rates. The promotion department will generally arrange for the displays at these conventions.

The promotional message is often carried directly by the editor or the publisher through speeches to industry groups at conventions, banquets, or elsewhere. Few opportunities bring the magazine closer to the people it wants to reach than to have a selected audience listen to the very people who produce the publication.

Publishers have begun to use radio and television and especially cable TV as promotional channels much more than they have in the past.

Public Relations and Publicity

To supplement, or complement, the work of the promotion department, many of the larger magazines use public relations to promote their activities. This is done through an in-house public relations department, an outside PR counsel, or, in a few cases, both.

Magazine PR is devoted to promoting the magazine. If a particular issue carries an article that is newsworthy, the PR department (or counsel) will see that newspapers, television news organizations, and newsmagazines receive the press releases and possibly a preprint of the article itself. The material need not be an important article. Anything in the magazine that might interest the broad general audience of newspaper readers, or the smaller audiences of specialty publications (sports, financial news, the arts, or whatever), offers a possibility of generating newspaper space through a pre-issue publicity release.

Another PR technique employed by magazines is the "media event." This is a party or a press conference to mark some event in the magazine's life—a birthday, the introduction of a new editor, or the publicizing of an important article by a celebrity who will draw newspaper, radio, and television reporters.

By far the most common device, however, is the press release, which is the bread-and-butter staple of PR work because it can be used in such a variety of ways. Local newspapers, for instance, always want to know about sons and daughters appearing in national magazines, for whatever reason. Any hard news about a magazine—the death of a famous editor or contributor, a lawsuit, or an attack by a political figure, to cite a few common examples—is always good for press releases to the wire services, which will produce national, and even international, publicity.

PART FOUR

RELATED FIELDS AND THE OUTLOOK FOR THE FUTURE

CHAPTER 13

RELATED FIELDS

Many people come into publishing without any previous experience or knowledge, while others enter it from related fields, bringing with them skills learned elsewhere. There is also a reverse flow, in which those who have learned skills in the publishing business go into related fields, usually because of the promise of more money and greater opportunity for advancement.

Since publishing is such a universal kind of occupation, almost anything learned elsewhere will be useful, just as there is nothing learned in school or college that will not ultimately benefit the learner.

Editorial techniques are the skills most easily translated from one field to another. People who learn to write and edit on a newspaper or magazine find that they can use these abilities in a book publisher's editorial department or in the publicity and promotion departments.

Next in ease of transition come production skills. The ability to lay out a magazine page is directly related to book layout and design, although less so to newspapers. Magazine and book production people are doing basically the same things, and there are many instances of designers and layout experts who have done well in both media.

Business and management people also find it relatively easy to move from one publishing field to another; their skills are needed in virtually every business, as we have earlier learned.

Promotion, publicity, and advertising people may find it somewhat more difficult to move laterally from book publishing, let us say, to newspaper or magazine work, but they, too, like almost everyone in the communications industry, are usually generalists. As for advertising sales reps, magazines and newspapers are always in need of topflight salespeople. Selling in the book business differs dramatically and is much more passive and low-key.

In short, movement within the three fields is both possible and quite logical. The newspaper, for example, has always been a training ground for the other media, as well as for writers of books. Many of the best American novelists of this century were newspeople in their youth, as were a large number of today's writers of popular fiction. In nonfiction alone, the books produced by journalists, former and present, would run into the thousands.

The magazine business, as we have pointed out, is larger and more varied in job possibilities than any of the other media, and for that reason alone, it is extremely attractive to newspaper and book people.

What are the salient differences among the three? Pace and pressure, obviously. Daily newspaper work has the tightest deadlines, followed by weekly newspapers and weekly magazines, especially newsmagazines, which must be almost as timely as newspapers. Monthly magazines are somewhat more leisurely; book publishing the most leisurely of all, but even in book publishing firms there are deadlines to be met. All three can be exhilarating at times, and boring at others. Of the three, magazines probably pay the highest salaries, but it is possible to earn a good living in any one of them.

The thing that unites the media is that they are all engaged in the dissemination of ideas, entertainment, and information. People select these media for a career because they like to work with the flow of ideas. The ultimate choice of which medium is usually determined more often by temperament than by opportunity. Thus there are people who have a lifelong preference for the routine way of life on newspapers, where patterns of writing are uniform.

Magazines are not so routinized; they are more innovative and they offer a broader latitude in writing. Newspaper publishers do not often succeed as magazine publishers, and vice versa. Newspaper workers, however, often do well on magazines, though the reverse is not generally as true. Magazine people who make the switch are often not happy with the change.

As for book publishing, it happily welcomes refugees from both newspaper and magazine work. And if you happen to land a job with one of the media giants, like Time-Warner or Newhouse, you will be working in a corporation that owns magazines and book publishing firms; in the case of Newhouse, newspapers as well.

PUBLIC RELATIONS AND ADVERTISING

Public relations (PR) and advertising, especially the former, attract many people from newspaper publishing.

Each year, public relations absorbs more and more graduates of journalism schools and departments. In fact, some colleges and universities have created a separate public relations department in response to student demand. Once again the reason for choosing PR over newspapers often is money, although the reports of what beginners and lower-echelon people are paid in PR often are highly exaggerated. Nevertheless, overall there is more money to be made in public relations than in working for newspapers, and there is also a great deal more variety.

Today, the field of public relations covers a wide area of human activity. There is the field of corporate public relations extending from the largest corporate giants to the smallest companies. Multinational business organizations have made this an international occupation, and the biggest companies have large public relations staffs. Then there are the public relations agencies, which service corporate and other clients, either handling their entire program or supplementing what their PR staff does. Major advertising agencies also have PR divisions that help with the problems of clients. Institutions of every kind, from universities to trade organizations, employ PR people, including government at every level, where the phrase "public relations" may not always be used, but the work is the same.

Magazine and book publishing people have also switched to PR work from time to time, as well as to advertising agencies. Once again, the criteria for success in these fields are the same as in publishing: creativity, writing ability, a facility for ideas, and the ability to communicate them.

TELEVISION AND RADIO

News broadcasting, both television and radio, is full of former newspaper reporters. Many network news executives started in the newspaper business, and the older generation of television news personalities has a newspaper background. There are fewer among the newer generation because the veterans came into television news at a time when it was new and badly in need of their expertise. Today, since it has become as much show business as it is news, it is quite possible for a young person to gain prominence by rising from the ranks of television itself, without any previous newspaper experience. Further, more colleges and universities now offer degrees in broadcast journalism, which focuses on radio and TV preparation.

Television news is organized in much the same way as a newspaper, and that is why the network news organizations in New York are so full of former *New York Times, Daily News,* and *Herald Tribune* employees, who may not be on-the-air personalities but who know how to get the news and write it. There are news directors who fulfill the same function as a newspaper's managing editor or city editor; writers who prepare the news that is read on the air from teleprompters or scripts; and reporters who go out on assignments with camera operators. The departure from similarity to newspaper work comes when these reporters do stand-ups, face the camera, and, half-memorizing or reading, or sometimes ad-libbing, make their verbal reports. In the office, they will also be doing voiceovers for whatever film is used, and they may appear on camera in the studio itself to introduce a film story or comment on it.

Radio always attracts a certain number of journalism graduates who seem to have an affinity for the kind of invisible visibility the medium provides. For all but the network radio news organizations and the activities of a relatively few metropolitan stations, radio news consists of five minutes of reading from the AP or UPI wire. Most stations (except the small independents) are affiliated with the networks, however, and they receive and broadcast the newscasts that emanate from New York City and Washington, DC. In some cases, networks use the voices of their television reporters on the radio. Since everything that goes on the air is read, no matter who reads it, radio stations and networks must employ staffs of writers and editors. It is to these jobs that newspaper reporters and editors are most apt to gravitate. The work is much the same, except for the special technique that goes into writing for a time space and the human voice, rather than for the printed page.

BOOK REVIEWING

Although very much a part of the community of the book, reviewers and critics should, like investigative journalists, necessarily remain slightly detached from the mainstream of publishing. If they are too closely involved with writers or publishers on a personal basis, it is difficult for them to maintain their objectivity, a quality all important in this field.

How do you become one? Most reviewers or book review editors of newspapers and magazines come to their jobs by way of newspaper reporting; at any rate, their main interests are in journalism. Books are considered newsworthy to most major newspapers and a handful of national magazines. A few reviewers are writers themselves. For those considering freelance reviewing, prospects are limited, and remuneration meager. Newspapers and magazines pay from as little as a "freebie," the free book, as payment, to $25 or $50 for a short review to $250 or $350 for a piece in *The New York Times Book Review. Publishers Weekly,* which runs several thousand short reviews a year, pays about $35 to $100 apiece for them. Another source of income from reviews is the *Kirkus Reviews,* a service much used by librarians and some booksellers. *Kirkus Reviews* is published bimonthly, runs some 4,500 reviews a year in advance of publication, and has been a source of pocket money for years for hundreds of recent college graduates looking for work in publishing.

Like the book industry as a whole, "the book review media continue to navigate a course between the pressures of commerce and the responsibility to our common culture" (*Books: The Culture & Commerce of Publishing*).

LIBRARIES

Although book publishing and librarianship are distinct though related fields, there is occasional movement from one to the other, usually from publishing to libraries. Infrequently, one hears of a librarian who comes to work for a publisher as a school and library counselor in the promotion department where that experience will be extremely useful.

CHAPTER 14

THE FUTURE OF PUBLISHING

Glendower: *I can call spirits from the vasty deep.*
Hotspur: *Why, so can I, or so can any man;*
　But will they come when you do call for them?
　　　—Henry IV, Part I

Rash indeed would be the person presuming to summon up the "Spirit of the Publishing Future." If book publishers, to take one example, only knew even what their next bestsellers were going to be, the business would be much simpler and better organized than it is. As it is, every publisher can tell you horror stories of the books turned down that later became big successes. Still, perhaps a few educated guesses can be made, based on present trends.

Book publishing has been in a long transition period during which the number of books being published has increased to more than sixty thousand titles a year—not all new books by any means, many of them being reprints or miscellaneous publications, but still adding substantially to the vexatious problem of distribution that has plagued the industry almost since it began.

The picture, though, is not all bleak. The American Booksellers Association estimates that the number of establishments in America today that sells books is in excess of 25,000. It is held that there are also more than 100,000 outlets for paperbacks.

Discounting has also made many hardcover books as attractive to buy as paperbacks. True, there is a price resistance to the hardcover title carrying a tag of $19.95 or more; but it used to be said that a hardcover book ought to cost as much as a ticket to a Broadway play. Anyone who recently has been in a Broadway theater knows that books are the better bargain. And there are books of every kind for every taste available in paperback–usually for prices between $3.50 and $12.00.

As for other outlets of distribution, there are more than 15,000 public libraries in the United States, 3,100 academic libraries, 50,000 viable school libraries, and some 12,000 to 20,000 special libraries. Altogether, the library market accounts for nearly $4 billion in book purchases each year. Wholesalers and retailers alike, thanks to the computer, are better organized than ever, and the book clubs, as reported earlier in this volume, have distributed millions of books to their members and continue to do so efficiently and prosperously.

Yet, that nagging problem of distribution will not go away. It is still hard to find a copy of an obscure reference book or volume of poetry or out-of-print classic. Publishers do not ordinarily care to fill single-copy orders and it can be weeks or months before a desired book can be obtained. However, the emerging e-book publishing scene, the Internet, the Net library, and the digitizing of old as well as new books may well change this.

New York publishing has also been passing from its traditional family-held character to a stage where it is either publicly held, part of a conglomerate, or a wholly owned subsidiary of a nonbook publishing corporation. In this new climate, the pressure to make all divisions of a house show a profit is great. Equally great is the pressure to eliminate, or at least reduce, the elements that show a loss.

In most instances, publishers have more or less successfully fended off these pressures, and there have been only a few cases where any kind of corporate pressure has been exerted as far as what may or may not be on the list is concerned. More common are the instances where corporate executives with no knowledge of book publishing have been sent to operate book house subsidiaries. Costly mistakes sometimes have been made by these executives, the interior atmospheres of some publishing houses have been changed, for the worse, and the trend has been to permit the profit ends to override the literary means. This trend, coupled with the economic slowdown of recent years, has had a depressing effect on the publishing of anything but those books that are reasonably assured of large sales. When fewer chances are taken, it is likely that fewer books of purely literary merit will be published. These problems will confront the next generation of publishers in a more acute form because it is unlikely that publishing, once infused with new capital, will ever go back to the old days when it was a cottage industry.

In any event, the curse of bigness is not one of publishing's pressing problems. Because of the emergence of so many small firms on the scene, each year now there has been an annual increase of 2.5 percent, net, of mergers and failures. As big business, book publishing is not up there with oil, automobiles, and foodstuffs. The whole book industry of the United States is smaller than the top seventy-five individual firms on *Fortune*'s 500 list.

There are other problems, however. One of the major ones is illiteracy. Several studies report that more than twenty-three million American adults are functionally illiterate and that the number is increasing by more than two million people a year. There is also much concern about what former Librarian of Congress Daniel Boorstin has called *aliteracy,* the ability to read coupled with the lack of desire to read. Still, as a Book Industry Study Group survey demonstrated, "about half of all adult Americans read books and their number is not declining." That is not a bad base on which to build the future of the book.

Publishing also has to contend increasingly with government in the struggle over copyright legislation. The complicating and threatening factor in this situation is the great change made first by copying machines and their use by libraries and by educators and subsequently by the availability of content posted online. Libraries and educators are united in their efforts to make printed materials available from books to the widest possible audiences through copying. Publishers and writers are united in trying to prevent what many of them see as the financial ruin of both if some kind of royalty system does not prevail for the copying of printed material, as it does in the case of musical performances. This is a complicated and emotional problem for the future, which may not be wholly resolved by whatever legislation is finally enacted.

Publishers also face the continuing threat of censorship, as they have since the first attempt at this was made by the courts in 1842. Censorship battles are being fought every day on federal, state, and local levels. The continuing and futile attempts of courts and legislatures to define obscenity have resulted in a crazy patchwork of laws across the country that defy rationality. The constant effort of courts and legislatures, backed by conservative pressure groups, is to suppress; the effort of the publishers, through their associations and legal counsel, is to fight them off in the name of the First Amendment, both through defensive action in the courts and lobbying in state legislatures and the Congress.

These same problems, illiteracy and aliteracy, affect newspapers and magazine publishers as well. Any serious decline in reading hurts the entire communications industry.

Newspapers and magazines, too, have both copyright and censorship problems. Newspapers have faced the threat of government censorship, as in the case of the Pentagon Papers and the *Washington Post.* Magazines such as *Penthouse* and *Playboy* have been judged obscene and removed from the newsstands. The copying of intellectual property obviously affects every arm of publishing.

THE COMPUTER AND ELECTRONIC PUBLISHING

"Cyberspace." "E-mail." "The Information Superhighway." "Internet." These are the buzzwords of the twentieth and early twenty-first centuries. What we are seeing is nothing less than a technological revolution, transforming all three publishing fields—books, newspapers, and magazines alike.

How Technologies Will Affect Publishing

The pace of technological change is affecting publishing in sweeping, often dramatic, ways. The ferment of technological progress today is the greatest it has been since the 1830s, and what it will mean eventually no one can accurately determine. All we can be certain of is that information and entertainment are going to be conveyed to readers in a variety of ways. Whether the book as a physical object, as we have known it since the fifteenth century, will survive is by no means certain. Most of the present generation of publishers would be aghast to think it might not, because for centuries the feel of a book in the hand has been an aesthetic enjoyment. But the next generation of publishers may find that the printed page can be transmitted to readers more easily and economically than its traditional bound form. In spite of warnings that the electronic media might replace books altogether, there seems to be an increase of interest in the page printed with pictures and text. A form that has survived for five centuries is not likely to disappear overnight, or perhaps at all, but the form of its transmission may well change.

Every new technology, from photography to television, has created new inducements to read books and magazines. Even books on audio and video cassettes can entice new readers. The computer itself has provided a highly popular subject for books and magazines. *Literary Market Place* lists some 150 publishers in the computer science field.

REFERENCE MATERIALS

For certain services the computer is much superior to the book: in providing speedy access to data that change frequently; in providing access to bibliographies and other information about the sources of knowledge or information; and for storage, retrieval, and preservation of graphic material. CD-ROM now makes it possible to re-create authentic reproductions of great works of art on a computer screen, accompanied by audio and video material enhancing the visual experience. The computer greatly facilitates the process of bringing out a book; in keeping sales, royalty and other records; and in producing frequent catalogs of new and backlist books. Now we even see "print-on-demand" systems that make it economical to publish shorter manuscripts or to reproduce out-of-print volumes for only a few potential readers. Many more miraculous devices probably await us.

And then there are some devices that are more like Frankenstein's monster, lurching out of the laboratory and terrifying the villagers. One such invention is the Ricoh Company's page-turning photocopying machine. Coupled with a digital scanner, this dazzling machine would make it possible to digitize a five-hundred-page book in less than an hour, without payment to either the author or the publisher. Should such digitized texts be posted on the Internet, thousands of additional illegal copies could be made. How then can intellectual property be protected?

A RAPIDLY CHANGING INDUSTRY

Many publishers seem undecided as to how to approach this new technology. Some have enthusiastically begun to enter the CD-ROM and DVD market themselves; others are leasing material to other producers. Retail booksellers sell CD-ROMs as they have sold audio books; a mixed media revolution has begun. "If you aren't part of the steamroller," one computer technologist has commented, "you'll be part of the road."

Will the book as a physical object disappear? Author Michael Crichton remarks: "Even computer people agree that we'll be reading print on paper for at least ten more years—which is an eternity in the computer world."

Therefore, we predict with some confidence—though not complete confidence—that the book will continue to coexist with these new technologies as vigorously as it has with all the other, earlier inventions that were expected to make it obsolete. However, these new technologies will have a profound influence in changing the character of book publishing.

"I cannot live without books," wrote Thomas Jefferson in a letter to John Adams. Most of us in publishing, and a great many ordinary readers, would have to say the same.

Trends in Newspaper Publishing

America has never been as dependent on newspapers as Europeans and people of other developed countries. The circulation of daily newspapers fell from sixty-two million in 1980 to sixty million in 1992, while the nation grew by approximately thirty million souls. The new population projections show America growing to 326 million by 2020. Will newspaper circulation continue to drop? Experts differ, but it is likely the trend will continue.

TECHNOLOGICAL CHANGES

One thing is certain about the communications business: Technology will continue to advance, as it has been doing for the past quarter-century. This advance has not been as rapid as many people predicted it would be, and that leads some observers to believe that the ultimate consequences may not occur nearly as soon as many of us thought. The reason for this is that while technology is capable of changing rapidly, human beings are not.

The major change in print media that has been occurring for some time is the introduction of computer technology in printing plants and mechanical departments, changing the way in which newspapers, magazines, and books are manufactured. It has been a process often marked by pain and confusion. In newspapers, for example, the coming of the completely automated composing room, predicted for so long, has been accelerated recently on major dailies, but at the cost of strikes, the disappearance of some papers, and constant struggles with unions. The use of computer terminals in the city room has changed the mechanical way in which stories are written, and electronic editing has brought the newsroom into synchronization with the composing room. The rapid advance of offset printing has changed the face of print media, and computer-set type is altering the appearance of both magazines and books, as well as newspapers—and not necessarily for the better, in the opinion of those who love typography. Whatever the costs, aesthetic and human economics have inexorably decreed these technological changes.

NEWSPAPERS ONLINE—THEN AND NOW

One early change was a kind of "electronic newspaper" that could be received in individual homes via home computer terminal or television set with a special attachment. The reader used these devices to select information from a centrally located computer database compiled and regularly updated by the newspaper. This electronic newspaper was called *videotext.*

There were two types of videotext. The first was called *viewdata,* which directly linked the reader to the central computer database by telephone line or cable television circuit. The reader used a keypad to select items for viewing.

The second system, *teletext,* made no direct connection to the central database. Instead, it used a standard TV signal to broadcast the information, which the reader accessed with a special decoder attached to the TV set and selected with a keypad as it passed by on the screen. Teletext was more limited than viewdata, but it was also less expensive.

For a reader who wished to have a paper copy of the information, it was possible to attach a printout device to the videotext receiver.

The advantages to both reader and newspaper are obvious. The reader does not have to wait for the paper but can have it on tap with its pages brought up-to-date regularly and the ability to take away any part desired. For the newspaper, it means removing at least part of the advantage television possesses, that is, timeliness in reporting the news. There is no way, of course, by which the chief advantage, live broadcasting of news events, can be overcome. But more than that, the financial savings to newspapers is enormous. Composing room, mailing room, and the present circulation system ultimately will no longer be needed.

This is only one of several projections communications experts have made in forecasting the future of newspapers. Technological development also continues in the areas of fiber optics, satellites, and new computer memory and storage devices. Whichever scenario one chooses to accept, however, the reality is by one technology or another, newspapers can be transmitted directly into the home from newspaper offices around-the-clock.

Other advances have been made. One hears of reporters calling in stories to machines that translate the voice into typed words that can then be rearranged and edited by computer. Electronics are beginning to transform a business that has changed more slowly than almost any other, and it will never be the same again.

The electronic newspaper is still in its infancy but is fast maturing, according to a report released by the Newspaper Association of America. In 1992, when the *Chicago Tribune* began Chicago Online, the first electronic newspaper on a national online service, there were about half a dozen less sophisticated independent computer services offered by newspapers.

By 1994 at least twenty-eight dailies were working in partnership with one of five national online services, such as America Online, Prodigy, and CompuServe. The papers included the *New York Times, Washington Post, Los Angeles Times,* and *Newsday.* Prodigy, for one, has an audience of about two million people. Newspapers have now joined the Internet, which has millions of users and grows every day.

Despite all this activity, however, most analysts say that newspapers have not yet figured out how to make money online—though they undoubtedly will solve this particular problem in the future. And advertisers, for example, still prefer to see their messages in print and, one suspects, so do readers. Students are advised to consult *Editor & Publisher* regularly and to stay tuned for further details.

The Magazine of the Future

The magazine of the future is already evident in the magazine of today. What we have seen in recent years, clearly, is increased specialization. Technology has made it possible to "tailor" a magazine for a specialized audience. A process called Seletronic harnesses the computer to the printing press and makes it possible to alter both the editorial and the advertising components of magazines to appeal to highly selective groups of readers. This system was first put to use by the Philadelphia-based *Farm Journal* to serve farmers in each of the different farm specialities, with editorial and advertising material geared to their interests.

Time magazine, too, experimented successfully with target marketing— pulling out the names, say, of 500,000 people who might be prospects of a certain new product. Then, using a computer-driven bindery line and ink-jet printer, the ad for that product carried a personal message to every subscriber receiving one of those 500,000 copies. Where will it all end? Nobody knows, or even dares to guess.

TODAY'S TECHNOLOGY

Computerized typesetting, actually done by editors on some magazines, is much cheaper than the nearly obsolete hot-metal type. Color separations using machines equipped with high-resolution scanners, computers, lasers, and other technical improvements can be produced with better quality and less cost than the old engravings. The desktop publishing revolution, originally scoffed at by the professional magazines, has become an integral part of many magazine production departments. The flexibility and instant "what-you-see-is-what-you-get" has enabled designers to fine-tune page layouts quickly and easily. The publishing systems used range from the personal desktop computer, which has enabled many small magazines to get off the ground, to multimillion-dollar systems like the Vista at *Time* magazine. It links the production department in New York to a worldwide satellite network for importing photographs and exporting finished pages electronically to printing plants.

Edwin Diamond, who was a noted media consultant and New York University professor, once taught a course at M.I.T. on inventions and gave this assignment to his engineering students: "Design a communications system that is lightweight and easily portable, yet has a capacity of 60,000 to 100,000 words. Display screen should be no more than 9 inches and fit flat on a desk top. System should have easy access so that even an eight-year-old can plug it in. Should be storable and recallable in seconds. Systems should be usable in airplanes, autos, and canoes. Cost should be no more than $3 a unit."

If the students succeed, of course, their invention would be the magazine.

Back in the 1970s, many futurists predicted the advent of a "paperless society." That society has not yet arrived, it probably never will. Although computers have radically changed life in most American business offices, they have not replaced the copying machine. The Xerox Corporation estimates that more than *500 billion* copies per year are produced around the world, while the American Paper Institute says that the market for commonly used office paper continues to grow at a 5 percent average annual rate.

The use of paper is growing because it is much easier and less expensive to produce copies than ever before. Some companies that attempted to become paperless have discovered that they have replaced memos with computer paper, and though the life cycle of a piece of paper may be shorter, most people are still used to hard copy.

"The paperless office is a fantasy as long as a perfect integration and wider networking of computers are not a reality," says Yuichi Murano, an assistant with Dataquest in Japan. "But networking is still in the early stages, and the extremely high cost of integrating systems does not yet justify itself in terms of higher returns."

THE INFORMATION SUPERHIGHWAY

As this book is going to press, most of us are traveling along the information superhighway and more and more computer users join the Internet all the time. In some cities, it is possible to get on the road without paying any dues.

The result, according to author Nicholson Baker in an op-ed piece in the *New York Times,* is that intellectual property "has become an opulent, sophisticated, even somewhat debauched region of the law." Nicholson then goes on to charge what he calls the "infohighwaymen" with appropriating copyrighted material without permission. Articles, essays, and book excerpts from *The Atlantic Monthly, The New Yorker,* and *Playboy* are among the many thousands of offerings available by fax or electronically for a fee from The Magazine Index, a service of Ziff Communications that is distributed on the Internet by the CARL Corporation. Copyright, in this brave new world, becomes virtually meaningless.

One solution to the problem, proposed by the National Writers Union, is a royalty-sharing plan modeled on the music industry's Ascap system. Whenever a magazine database downloads or faxes an article to a consumer, some percentage of the fee charged trickles down to the person who wrote the piece. A writer should certainly have a say in determining who will sell his or her words, in what format, and at what price. Sounds fair enough.

WHAT'S NEXT?

For decades, now, we have been hearing that the day was rapidly approaching when people would sit in their living rooms before consoles and television screens and summon printed matter—newspaper, books, and magazines—before their eyes, paying for them electronically and never having to stir from their homes. WebTV comes close to this prophecy. Similarly, business would be done at home, and workers would no longer have to commute to their no-longer-needed offices. Everyone would be accessible to everyone else through the electronic world. The technology now exists, for the most part, to bring this staggering revolution about.

Will it happen? Thousands of people in the media business shudder at even the possibility—the entire distribution system wiped out, a large category of occupations rendered obsolete. Then reason takes over. What about the millions upon millions of people who are in motion from one place to another, on airplanes, trains, and buses? Many of them are reading as they travel, having purchased some kind of printed matter before boarding.

The futurists have an answer for that one. There are already in existence lap readers, devices that can be carried about like thin attaché cases, and opened up to reveal a screen on one side and a device for microfiches or DVD on the other. The microfiche, a miracle of reduction photography, can encompass an entire book or even several books on a single thin card or set of cards. Inserted in a reader, the page-by-page image flashes on the screen. Laptop computers, a more recent innovation, allow the user to "read" a book-length manuscript or the contents of a magazine, including photographs, contained on a single disk. Even newer developments with CD-I technology, which stands for Compact Disk-Interactive, give us video-type magazines complete with living color, text, still and motion pictures, and CD-quality stereo sound.

Whether we will adapt our reading habits to this new technology on a massive scale remains a disputed question. Whether people will learn with eagerness to abandon the easy mobility of the newspaper, magazine, or book held in the hand for the mechanical reproducing system remains to be seen.

PROFESSIONAL ASSOCIATIONS

Most professional associations provide career information and many offer job locating services. A letter, an e-mail, or a visit to a website will bring you in contact with a wealth of leads in your areas of interest.

The following is just a sampling of key associations. Your own Internet search will bring you hundreds more.

BOOKS

American Booksellers Association
Information Service Center
828 S. Broadway
Tarrytown, NY 10591
E-mail: info@bookweb.org
http://www.ambook.org/

Association of American Publishers (AAP)
50 F St. NW
Washington, DC 20001
71 Fifth Ave.
New York, NY 10013
http://publishing.miningco.com/
business/publishing/gi/dynamic/
offsite.htm?site=http://
www.publishers.org/

Association of American University Presses (AAUP)
The Association of American
University Presses, Inc.
71 W. 23rd St., Suite 901
New York, NY 10010
http://aaup.princeton.edu/

The Association of Authors' Representatives, Inc. (AAR)
P. O. Box 237201 Ansonia Station
New York, NY 10003
http://www.publishersweekly.com/aar/

The Association of Canadian Publishers
110 Eglinton Ave. W., Suite 401
Toronto, ON M4R 1A3
Canada
E-mail: info@canbook.org
http://publishing.miningco.com/
business/publishing/gi/dynamic/
offsite.htm?site=http://
www.publishers.ca/

The Association of Electronic Publishers
http://welcome.to/AEP

The Audio Publishers Association
627 Aviation Way
Manhattan Beach, CA 90266
http://www.audiopub.org/

Canadian Publishers' Council
250 Merton St., Suite 203
Toronto, ON M4S 1B1
Canada
http://publishing.miningco.com/
business/publishing/gi/dynamic/
offsite.htm?site=http://
www.pubcouncil.ca/
E-mail: pubadmin@pubcouncil.ca

National Association of Independent Publishers
P. O. Box 430
Highland City, FL 33846–0430
E-mail: NAIP@aol.com
http://publishing.miningco.com/
business/publishing/gi/dynamic/
offsite.htm?site=http://lcweb.
loc.gov/loc/cfbook/coborg/nai.html

National Association of Publisher Representatives
399 E. 72nd St., Suite 3F
New York, NY 10021

Publisher's Weekly
http://www.publishersweekly.com/

NEWSPAPERS

American Newspaper Publishers Association
The Newspaper Center
11600 Sunrise Valley Dr.
Reston, VA 22091

American Society of Media Photographers
14 Washington Rd., Suite 502
Princeton Junction, NJ 08550

American Society of Newspaper Editors
P.O. Box 4090
Reston, VA 22090–1700

Associated Press Broadcasters Association
1825 K St. NW, Suite 710
Washington, DC 20006

The Dow Jones Newspaper Fund
P.O. Box 300
Princeton, NJ 08543–0300

Investigative Reporters and Editors
100 Neff Hall
University of Missouri
Columbia, MO 65211

National Newspaper Association
1525 Wilson Blvd.
Arlington, VA 22209
For career information and a pamphlet titled "Newspaper Careers and Challenges for the Next Century"

National Press Photographers Association
3200 Cloasdaile Dr., Suite 306
Durham, NC 27705

The Newspaper Guild
8611 Second Ave.
Silver Springs, MD 20910

Radio and Television News Directors Association
1717 K St. NW, Suite 615
Washington, DC 20006

MAGAZINES

American Society of Magazine Editors
919 Third Ave.
New York, NY 10022

Council of Literary Magazines and Presses
E-mail: CLMPNYC@aol.com
http://publishing.miningco.com/
business/publishing/gi/dynamic/
offsite.htm?site=http://
www.litline.org/html/clmp.html

Magazine Publishers of America
919 Third Ave.
New York, NY 10022
1211 Connecticut Ave. NW
Washington, DC 20036
http://publishing.about.com/business/
publishing/msub1a.htm

Society of National Association Publications
1150 Connecticut Ave. NW, Suite 1050
Washington, DC 20036
Publications owned or operated by
professional associations and
societies
For magazine jobs
http://publishing.about.com/business/
publishing/msubmagazinejobs.htm

WRITERS

American Society of Journalists and Authors
1501 Broadway, Suite 302
New York, NY 10036

Author's League of America
330 W. 42nd St., 29th Floor
New York, NY 10036

Fiction Writer's Connection (FWC)
P.O. Box 72300
Albuquerque, NM 87195
E-mail: Bcamenson@aol.com
http://www.fictionwriters.com

National Conference of Editorial Writers
6223 Executive Blvd.
Rockville, MD 20852

Society for Technical Communication, Inc.
901 N. Stuart St., Suite 904
Arlington, VA 22203

PREPARATORY PROGRAMS FOR THE BOOK TRADE

The following is a sampling of the many institutions offering courses and programs in the different areas of the publishing field. To locate current addresses, phone numbers, and websites, do an Internet search or refer to any of the college directories, available in public libraries.

Arizona State University
Creative Writing Program

Arkansas State University
Printing Program

Association of Graphic Communications
Graphic Arts Education Center

Baylor University
Writing Program

Binghamton University
Writing Program

Boston University
Graduate Creative Writing Program

Bowling Green State University
Creative Writing Program

Center for Book Arts
Bookbinding, printing, and papermaking
    workshops

Chicago Book Clinic Seminars
Seminars for publishers

Childworks Agency
White Pines National Conference for
    Writers and Illustrators of Children's
    Books

Columbia University School of the Arts
Writing Division

Dynamic Graphics Educational
    Foundation
Professional workshops and seminars

Emerson College
Writing and Publishing Program

Fiction Writer's Connection
Writing for Publication Program

Fordham University
Graduate School of Business
    Administration

George Washington University
Center for Career Education

Graphic Arts Guild New York
Business workshops and seminars

H. H. Herbert School of Journalism &
    Mass Communication
Professional Writing Program

Hamilton College
English/Creative Writing

Harvard University
Radcliffe Publishing Course

Hofstra University
English Department

Hollins College
Writing Program

Louisiana State University
Writing Program

McNeese State University
Writing Program

Massachusetts College of Art
Writing Children's Literature

Mississippi Review/University of Southern
    Mississippi
Center for Writers

Mystery Writers of America, Inc.
Writing Workshops

The National Writer's Voice Project
The Writer's Voice of New York

New York City Technical College
Center for Advertising, Printing, and
    Publishing

New York University
Center for Publishing

Oberlin College
Creative Writing Program

Ohio University
English Department, Creative Writing
    Program

Pace University
Master of Science in Publishing

Parsons School of Design
Design courses

Rice University Continuing Studies
Rice University Publishing Program

Rochester Institute of Technology
School of Printing

School of Visual Arts
New York

Stanford University
Stanford Professional Publishing Course

Syracuse University
Creative Writing Program

Syracuse University
Newhouse School of Public
    Communications

University of Alabama
Program in Creative Writing

University of Baltimore—Yale Gordon
    College of Liberal Arts
Institute for Language, Technology, and
    Publications Design

University of California Extension
Certificate Program in Publishing and
    Professional Sequence in Copyediting

University of Chicago
Graham School of General Studies

The University of Connecticut
The Realities of Publishing

University of Denver
Publishing Institute

University of Hawaii
Manoa Writing Program

University of Houston
Creative Writing Program

University of Illinois at Chicago
Program for Writers

University of Illinois
Department of Journalism

University of Iowa
Writer's Workshop, Graduate Creative
    Writing Program

University of Missouri-Kansas City
New Letters Weekend Writers Conference

University of Montana
Environmental Writing Institute

University of Pennsylvania
College of General Studies Special
    Programs

University of Southern California
Professional Writing Program

University of Texas at Austin
Writing Program

University of Texas at El Paso
Writing Program

University of Virginia
Publishing and Communications Program

University of Wisconsin
Madison Communication Programs

Vermont College
M.F.A Writing Program

Warren Wilson College
M.F.A Program for Writers

Washington University
The Writing Program

Writer's Digest School
Correspondence courses